THE HAMLYN LECTURES
FORTY-SEVENTH SERIES

FROM THE TEST TUBE TO THE COFFIN
Choice and Regulation in Private Life

AUSTRALIA
LBC Information Services—Sydney

CANADA and USA
Carswell—Toronto

NEW ZEALAND
Brooker's—Auckland

SINGAPORE and MALAYSIA
Thomson Information (S.E. Asia)—Singapore

FROM THE TEST TUBE TO THE COFFIN
Choice and Regulation in Private Life

by

BRENDA HALE
The Hon. Mrs Justice Hale D.B.E.,
formerly Professor Brenda Hoggett,
Law Commissioner

Published under the auspices of
THE HAMLYN TRUST

LONDON
STEVENS & SONS/SWEET & MAXWELL
1996

Published in 1996 by Sweet & Maxwell Limited of
100 Avenue Road, Swiss Cottage,
London NW3 3PF
Typeset by Selwood Systems,
Midsomer Norton
Printed in England by
Clays Ltd, St Ives plc

No natural forests were destroyed to make this product;
only farmed timber was used and replanted

**A CIP catalogue record for this book is available from the British
Library**

ISBN 0 421 582 707 (HB)
0 421 582 804 (PB)

TABLE OF CONTENTS

Acknowledgements   vii
The Hamlyn Lectures   ix
The Hamlyn Trust   xiii
Preface   xv

1.   Introduction   1
2.   Hatchings   4
3.   Matchings   45
4.   Dispatchings   87
5.   Resumé   123

ACKNOWLEDGEMENTS

The Publishers and author wish to acknowledge the permission of the following to reproduce the cartoons used in this book:

On pages 5 and 119, "Well yes, actually I *do* want to be a burden, son" and "I need to know whether he's worth more dead or alive, and if the latter, married or divorced" – © Roger Beale. Every effort has been made to contact the cartoonist to request permission to reproduce these cartoons, but without success.

On page 29, "Mummy, where do Daddies come from?" – © Michael Heath

On page 54, "Look it up – nobody knows what it means" – © Pugh/The Times, 1995

On page 65, "We want one of those old-fashioned acrimonious divorces" – © The Telegraph plc, London, 1996

On pages 69 and 86, "He's the mediator for Mum and Dad's 'no fault' divorce . . ." and "The Law Commission has come up with a wonderful solution . . ." – © Mac of the Daily Mail

On page 80, "Marriage?? Isn't that some kind of pre-divorce agreement?" – © Merrily Harpur

THE HAMLYN LECTURES

1949   Freedom under the Law
      by the Rt. Hon. Lord Denning

1950   The Inheritance of the Common Law
      by Richard O'Sullivan, Esq.

1951   The Rational Strength of English Law
      by Professor F.H. Lawson

1952   English Law and the Moral Law
      by Professor A.L. Goodhart

1953   The Queen's Peace
      by Sir Carleton Kemp Allen

1954   Executive Discretion and Judicial Control
      by Professor C.J. Hamson

1955   The Proof of Guilt
      by Professor Glanville Williams

1956   Trial by Jury
      by the Rt. Hon. Lord Devlin

1957   Protection from Power under English Law
      by the Rt. Hon. Lord MacDermott

1958   The Sanctity of Contracts in English Law
      by Professor Sir David Hughes Parry

1959   Judge and Jurist in the Reign of Victoria
      by C.H.S. Fifoot, Esq.

The Hamlyn Lectures

1960   The Common Law in India
      by M.C. Setalvad, Esq.

1961   British Justice: The Scottish Contribution
      by Professor Sir Thomas Smith

1962   Lawyer and Litigant in England
      by the Rt. Hon. Sir Robert Megarry

1963   Crime and the Criminal Law
      by the Baroness Wootton of Abinger

1964   Law and Lawyers in the United States
      by Dean Erwin N. Griswold

1965   New Law for a New World?
      by the Rt. Hon. Lord Tangley

1966   Other People's Law
      by the Rt. Hon. Lord Kilbrandon

1967   The Contribution of English Law to South African
      Law: and the Rule of Law in South Africa
      by the Hon. O.D. Schreiner

1968   Justice in the Welfare State
      by Professor H. Street

1969   The British Tradition in Canadian Law
      by the Hon. Bora Laskin

1970   The English Judge
      by Henry Cecil

1971   Punishment, Prison and the Public
      by Professor Sir Rupert Cross

1972   Labour and the Law
      by Professor Sir Otto Kahn-Freund

The Hamlyn Lectures

1973 Maladministration and its Remedies
by Sir Kenneth Wheare

1974 English Law—The New Dimension
by the Rt. Hon. Lord Scarman

1975 The Land and the Development; or, The Turmoil
and the Torment
by Sir Desmond Heap

1976 The National Insurance Commissioners
by Sir Robert Micklewait

1977 The European Communities and the Rule of Law
by Lord Mackenzie Stuart

1978 Liberty, Law and Justice
by Professor Sir Norman Anderson

1979 Social History and Law Reform
by Professor Lord McGregor of Durris

1980 Constitutional Fundamentals
by Professor Sir William Wade

1981 Intolerable Inquisition? Reflections on the Law of
Tax
by Hubert Monroe

1982 The Quest for Security: Employees, Tenants,
Wives
by Professor Tony Honoré

1983 Hamlyn Revisited: The British Legal System
Today
by Lord Hailsham of St. Marylebone

1984 The Development of Consumer Law and Policy—
Bold Spirits and Timorous Souls
by Sir Gordon Borrie

1985   Law and Order
      by Professor Ralf Dahrendorf

1986   The Fabric of English Civil Justice
      by Sir Jack Jacob

1987   Pragmatism and Theory in English Law
      by P.S. Atiyah

1988   Justification and Excuse in the Criminal Law
      by J.C. Smith

1989   Protection of the Public—A New Challenge
      by the Rt. Hon. Lord Justice Woolf

1990   The United Kingdom and Human Rights
      by Dr. Claire Palley

1991   Introducing a European Legal Order
      by Gordon Slynn

1992   Speech & Respect
      by Professor Richard Abel

1993   The Administration of Justice
      by Lord Mackay of Clashfern

1994   Blackstone's Tower: The English Law School
      by Professor William Twining

1995   From the Test Tube to the Coffin: Choice and
      Regulation in Private Life
      by the Hon. Mrs Justice Hale

THE HAMLYN TRUST

The Hamlyn Trust owes its existence to the will of the late Miss Emma Warburton Hamlyn of Torquay, who died in 1941 at the age of 80. She came of an old and well-known Devon family. Her father, William Bussell Hamlyn, practised in Torquay as a solicitor and J.P. for many years, and it seems likely that Miss Hamlyn founded the trust in his memory. Emma Hamlyn was a woman of strong character, intelligent and cultured, well-versed in literature, music and art, and a lover of her country. She travelled extensively in Europe and Egypt, and apparently took considerable interest in the law and ethnology of the countries and cultures that she visited. An account of Miss Hamlyn by Dr Chantal Stebbings of the University of Exeter may be found, under the title "The Hamlyn Legacy," in volume 42 of the published lectures.

Miss Hamlyn bequeathed the residue of her estate on trust in terms which it seems were her own. The wording was thought to be vague, and the will was taken to the Chancery Division of the High Court, which in November 1948 approved a Scheme for the administration of the trust. Paragraph 3 of the Scheme, which closely follows Miss Hamlyn's own wording, is as follows:

"The object of the charity is the furtherance by lectures or otherwise among the Common People of the United Kingdom of Great Britain and Northern Ireland of the knowledge of the Comparative Jurisprudence and Ethnology of the Chief European countries including the United Kingdom, and the circumstances of the growth of such jurisprudence to the Intent that the Common People of the United Kingdom may realise the privileges which in law and custom they enjoy in comparison with other European Peoples and realising and appreciating such privileges may recognise the responsibilities and obligations attaching to them."

The Trustees are to include the Vice-Chancellor of the University of Exeter, representatives of the Universities of London, Leeds,

Glasgow, Belfast and Wales and persons co-opted. At present there are nine Trustees:

From the outset it was decided that the Trust's objects could best be achieved by means of an annual course of public lectures of outstanding interest and quality by eminent Lecturers, and by their subsequent publication and distribution to a wider audience. Details of these Lectures are given on page ix. In recent years, however, the Trustees have expanded their activities by organising supplementary regional lecture tours and by setting up a "small grants" scheme to provide financial support for other activities designed to further public understanding of the law.

The forty-seventh series of lectures was intended to be delivered by the Hon. Mrs Justice Hale at the Queen's University of Belfast in November 1995. For reasons outside our control it was eventually delivered in Belfast and at King's College, London, in May 1996.

September 1996   DESMOND GREER
                                               Chairman of the Trustees

PREFACE

This little book was first planned as a series of lectures to be delivered at the Queen's University of Belfast in the Autumn term of 1995. Lecturing has been my trade for most of my professional life and I was looking forward to it. The aim was to draw together the threads of a varied experience in university and public life and see whether they made any sense. Then events conspired against us. In January 1994, I became a High Court Judge after nearly 10 years as a Law Commissioner: this broadened my experience but narrowed the options about what I could say and when I could say it. In October 1995, two of my projects at the Law Commission suddenly became politically controversial in an unexpected way. Then in November 1995, the President of the United States decided to visit, not only Belfast but also the Queen's University, just when the lectures were due to be given. That is why the 1995 Hamlyn Lectures were eventually delivered in 1996. It also why a book which set out to examine the Family Law Act 1996 before it was even introduced into Parliament is now being published after it has become law. Perhaps that is just as well. But I hope that the design for a live performance manages to survive. It has been a great pleasure, and a great honour, to give the forty-seventh series of lectures—only the third time by a woman and the first to concentrate on the field of private and family life. I am grateful to Miss Hamlyn and her trustees for making it possible.

Brenda Hale
August 23, 1996

1. Introduction

Miss Hamlyn wanted the people of the United Kingdom to understand the "privileges which in law and custom they enjoy in comparison with other European peoples". She also hoped that this would make us understand the responsibilities and obligations attaching to those privileges. She must have had in mind, amongst other things, the privileges of democracy and freedom. She died in 1941 in the midst of a war being fought to save those privileges from the darker forces of tyranny and oppression.

But there is one area of human activity in which the law has traditionally been reluctant to give us freedom and equality. This is in our private and family lives: having a child, making and breaking our intimate relationships, and ending our lives. Even in 1941, the law did not allow us a free choice in these things. Children had to be born within marriage or else they could largely be ignored. Heterosexual relationships had to be conducted within marriage or else the adults would have no responsibility for one another. The law laid down what marriage meant and the couple had little choice but to accept it. It still meant very different things for men and for women. Male homosexual relationships were prohibited altogether. And few people were left in charge of how and when they would die.

All of this has changed a great deal since then and in particular over the last quarter century or so. There are now many more choices legally available to us in the conduct of our private and family lives, and a much greater freedom to choose between them. But there are also many more children being born outside marriage, fewer or at least later marriages, much more divorce, many more parents bringing up their children alone, more couples living together outside marriage, and much else for the community to worry about. There are the psychological, social and economic effects of all this on the people involved, and especially the children, but there are also effects on the community at large.

1

Introduction

I want to examine how and why the law has got to its present position: why it has mostly abandoned the old machinery for regulating our private and family lives, and we are now puzzled about what can and should be put in its place. I shall be more concerned with the civil than the criminal law. This is not to deny the importance of the well-known debates about the use of the criminal law in the enforcement of morals: but punishment is only one, comparatively simple, way in which the law tries to control our behaviour. The law which regulates whether and how we can have a child, what sorts of arrangements we can make with our lovers, and the deals we can do with death and the doctor covers a much wider field. It operates in a much more subtle and complicated fashion.

I shall also have to ignore the ways in which taxation and social policies affect these areas of our lives. Sometimes they intend to do so, when they give advantages to married couples or refuse to give advantages to the unmarried; sometimes the effect is unintended; often it is contradictory. But their principal purpose is something different; tax laws are there to raise money, benefit laws are there to abolish want. I an concerned with the laws which deliberately set out to control our private and family lives. The more that these allow or insist that we take responsibility for one another and for our children, the less the State will have to do so.

Most of these laws can loosely be called "family law", a subject which has been hardly touched on at all in the previous 46 years of Hamlyn lectures. Yet it fits Miss Hamlyn's purpose very well. The family laws of western Europe are still very different from one another; religion and the influence of Roman law play a part in this. But they are moving closer together. Shortly after the Second World War the Council of Europe was formed and the European Convention on Human Rights was concluded. This has several articles which try to protect our private and family lives. This is one reason why family law now allows us much greater freedom of choice than once it did. But there is no reason why that privilege should not bring with it proper responsibilities and obligations.

Law and life do not always arrange themselves into the same tidy parcels. Family life has traditionally been punctuated and defined by three ceremonials: baptisms, weddings and funerals, colloquially known to many as "hatchings", "matchings" and "dispatchings". Whatever else may change, the events which they

2

mark are still and will always be the three great milestones along the way.

The law does not arrange itself in the same neat fashion. It also approaches each of these subjects in a rather different way. The first two are now mostly governed by statute law which gives a good deal of discretion to courts and others to decide what will be best. The last is mainly governed by case law which is still working out the balance between rules and discretion. But the subject is so sensitive that it looks as though the courts will have to continue to do this without Parliamentary help for some time to come.

2. Hatchings

Late one Friday afternoon in September 1995 I was asked for an injunction to protect six young children from further press harassment and publicity. Prompted by the BBC "Today" programme, the tabloids had whipped themselves into a frenzy of indignation. The mother, "Sarah", had six children by four different fathers. None of the children were living with her. All were entirely dependent on the State. She had married a "Schedule 1 offender"[1] and reportedly wanted a sterilisation operation reversed so that she could have yet more children. She was, in Polly Toynbee's words, one of a "parade of single parents from hell; that handful of women with multiple children by different fathers who see no reason why the taxpayer should not pay."[2]

What were the media so frightened about? Was it that "Sarah" was having children by so many different partners, in and outside marriage? Or that she was having children she could not afford to keep? Or that she was having children when she was unfit to look after them properly? Or that she was now looking for medical help to enable her to have more? Despite her reported claim that "there are thousands of women like me",[3] there are not many who are quite like her.

Do people like Sarah have the right to go on having children whenever and however they choose? The right *not* to have a child has been debated hard and long, and I have no wish to add to that debate. Much less has been said about the right to have one, still less about the right to choose what sort of child to have.

---

[1] Schedule 1 to the Children and Young Persons Act 1933 lists most offences of a sexual, violent or cruel nature towards children; before the Children Act 1989, the presence of such a person in the household was one of only two circumstances in which care proceedings could be brought because of probable rather than actual harm, under the Children and Young Persons Act 1969, s. 1(2)(bb).
[2] "Why single mothers baffle Mr Lilley," *The Independent*, October 11, 1995.
[3] See "There are thousands of women like me," *Daily Mail*, September 25, 1995.

4

THE RIGHT TO HAVE A CHILD?

We all have an interest in the quantity and the quality of the next generation. Individually, we want the joys as well as the pains of parenthood, someone to care about us in our old age, and to pass on our genes and whatever property or status we may have. Collectively, we want to preserve our community, our society and our culture. We need enough younger people to protect us all, and to look after and provide for the increasing numbers of old and very old people. So we need enough children, ready, willing and able to carry on after us, but we also need them to be healthy, properly cared for and properly brought up.

By Roger Beale

These are world-wide needs, but they can only be protected and enforced through national laws. At one extreme, we might try to license parenthood itself, regulating who may have children, and providing in detail for how they are to be brought up. We might even couple this with a compulsory element, requiring certain particularly suitable people to reproduce. At the other extreme, we might allow complete freedom of choice about whether to have a child, how to do so, and how to bring them up. We might even couple this with a duty to supply the means of doing so to whoever wanted it. The answer in practice and in principle must lie somewhere in between these two extremes.

There are strong arguments in favour of some regulation.[4] Bearing and rearing children is an extremely harmful activity if done badly. Harm is done to the children themselves, through ill-treatment, neglect or unhappiness in childhood and their possible ill-effects in adult life. Harm is done to the rest of us, who have to protect both the children and ourselves from the consequences, and may lose the expected benefits of the new generation. That harm could be reduced, if not entirely avoided, if some minimal standard of competence could be established in advance. Other activities which are beneficial if done well but harmful if done badly have to be licensed, so why not this?

All the practical and theoretical arguments against this idea come tumbling to mind. They go hand in hand; the practical steps which would be necessary to make sense of such a system are incompatible with the underlying values and principles of our laws.

First, the State cannot prevent all unlicensed conceptions in advance. A licensing system could only be enforced after the event by a combination of criminal penalties against the parents and automatic removal of the child. These would often harm the very people it was trying to protect. This objection does not apply with quite the same force to people who want or need professional help in order to have a child; they could simply be denied that help. Even then, with such a desirable commodity, we might expect a black market or other evasive devices to develop.

Secondly, even if a licensing system could be enforced, by sacrificing a few children to encourage other would-be parents, how likely is it that we could devise sufficiently accurate ways of testing in advance the parenting capacity and commitment of each individual who wanted to try? The experience of trying to do this in the contest of adoption and fostering is not particularly encouraging.[5] We cannot validate this experience scientifically through controlled experiments. The adoption of young babies by committed strangers has turned out remarkably well; but there is not a great deal of evidence that careful professional selection produces better outcomes than more random private arrangements.[6] Choosing a new family for an existing child is

---

[4] H. Lafollette, "Licensing Parents" (1980) 9 *Philosophy and Public Affairs* 182.
[5] E. Blyth, "Assisted Reproduction: what's in it for the children?" (1990) 4 *Children and Society* 167.
[6] *e.g.* the experiences of the National Child Development Study of all children born in one week in 1958, reported in J. Lambert and J. Streather, *Children in Changing*

quite different from choosing in advance who may have a child of their own. Once again, we could at least try to test those who need help, even if we cannot test those who proceed in the normal way.

This leads to the objections of principle. The rights set out in Articles 8 to 12 of the European Convention on Human Rights form a coherent and inter-related group: the right to respect for private and family life, home and correspondence; the right to freedom of expression; the right to freedom of peaceful assembly and free association; and the right to marry and found a family. These are the very essentials of a free-thinking and free-speaking society. Bringing up one's own family in one's own way is part of that. The point was summed up by the Review of Child Care Law in 1985:

"... it is important in a free society to maintain the rich diversity of lifestyles which is secured by permitting families a large measure of autonomy in the way in which they bring up their children."[7]

Article 12 is a little different from the others:

"Men and women of marriageable age have the right to marry and to found a family, according to the national laws governing the exercise of this right."

Articles 8 to 11 all allow for exceptions which are "necessary in a democratic society" for certain purposes; but there are no exceptions to Article 12. States can regulate how people get married.[8] But they must not discriminate in the kinds of people to whom they make this right available. Article 14 provides:

"The enjoyment of the rights and freedoms set forth in this Convention shall be secured without discrimination on any ground such as sex, race, colour, language, religion, political or other opinion, national or social origin, association with a national minority, property, birth or other status."

Families: A Study of Adoption and Illegitimacy (1980, Macmillan), and J. Seglow, M. Kellmer Pringle and P. Wedge, *Growing Up Adopted* (1972, National Foundation for Educational Research).
[7] DHSS, *Review of Child Care Law: Report to ministers of an interdepartmental working party*, published by the Government as a Consultative Document, September 1985, para. 2.13.
[8] European Commission, *X. v. Federal Republic of Germany*: Application 6167/73; (1975) 1 D. & R. 64.

The Convention was formulated in the context of revulsion against the eugenic policies and practices of the Third Reich. People should not be discriminated against because of their membership of an identifiable group. Everyone is entitled to be considered as an individual. This does not prevent States setting qualifications for marriage provided that individuals retain the right to have their qualifications properly assessed.

The right to marry and found a family, however, is one right, not two. Men and women of marriageable age must be allowed to marry and to have at least one child if they wish, but for the time being at least, unmarried people do not have the same right. This was "almost certainly" the original intention.[9] The object was to protect individuals' rights to found a family within the conventional institutional structure.[10] But the right of unmarried people to have children may well be an aspect of their private lives which is entitled to respect under Article 8:

"1. Everyone has the right to respect for his private and family life, his home and his correspondence.

2. There shall be no interference by a public authority with the exercise of this right except such as is in accordance with the law and is necessary in a democratic society in the interests of national security, public safety or the economic well-being of the country, for the prevention of disorder or crime, for the protection of health or morals, or for the protection of the rights and freedoms of others."

But it is one thing to respect a person's freedom to have children if he or she can. It is quite another thing to give them a right to be supplied with the children they are unable or unwilling to have for themselves in the usual way. We only need to think of this in the context of the usual methods of reproduction to recognise its absurdity: the mind boggles at the prospect of a national stud or surrogacy service. The fact that assisted reproductive techniques have separated conception and childbearing from sexual intercourse should make no difference. The State cannot have a duty to supply a service on demand. Would-be parents may, however, be entitled to expect fair treatment from those who

[9] P. van Dijk and G.J.H. van Hoof, *Theory and Practice of the European Convention on Human Rights* (2nd ed. 1990, Kluwer), p. 448.
[10] It is turning this reasoning on its head to say that therefore only those who are able to found a family are able to marry, but see *Rees v. U.K.* Series A No. 106; (1986) 9 E.H.R.R. 56.

allocate what the State does supply or who regulate what others will supply either voluntarily or for reward.

There could be other limits upon the freedom to have children. Should one, for example, be free intentionally (or even recklessly) to create children without incurring any subsequent responsibility towards them? Or to create children with a view to ill-treating or neglecting them? It can easily be argued that a person only "has the right to rear children if he meets certain minimal standards of child rearing. Parents must not abuse or neglect their children and must also provide for the basic needs of the children."[11] But we must be careful not to confuse the right to bear children with the right to rear them: we may be justified in trying to enforce child support and other parental responsibilities, to provide a better life for abused and neglected children, and to punish the abusers. It does not follow that we are entitled to prevent their having children in the first place.

I will suggest, therefore, that we neither can nor should try to control in advance the freedom to have children in the normal way; but that we can try to regulate the supply of children to people who do not or cannot have them in the normal way, for the sake of the children themselves as well as the wider community; and that we can, of course, try to ensure that all parents honour their obligations to the children they have brought into the world, and rescue their children if they do not.

CHOOSING TO HAVE A CHILD

The range of choices available, as to whether and in what social circumstances to have children, and even what children to have, has increased dramatically in recent years. Not everyone will be happy with the results.

Fewer women are having children.[12] Those who do are having fewer children. They are also having them later in life: women in their early thirties are now more likely to have a child than women in their early twenties.[13] The total period fertility rate[14] in the United Kingdom is higher than anywhere else in the

---

[11] Lafollette, *op. cit.*, at p. 187.

[12] Central Statistical Office, *Social Trends 25* (1995), Chart 2.22: Percentage of women childless at age 30 and 40.

[13] *Social Trends 26*, Table 2.22: Fertility rates: by age.

[14] *i.e.* giving the average number of children per woman if current rates remain the same throughout her child-bearing years.

1.11

Total period fertility rate¹

United Kingdom
Rates

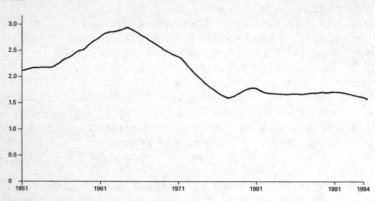

1 The average number of children which would be born per woman if women experienced the age specific fertility rates
of the period in question throughout their child-bearing lifespan
Source: Social Trends 26 (1996).Crown copyright 1996 Reproduced by permission of the Controller of HMSO and the
Office for National Statistics.

European Union apart from the Irish Republic,[15] but it fell sharply
from a peak in 1964 until 1977, when it levelled off some-
what.[16] At 1.75 in 1994 it is now well below replacement level of
2.1.

Over the same sort of period, the proportion of births outside
marriage has shot up, from just over five per cent in 1960 to over
32 per cent in 1994.[17] This, too, is amongst the highest in the
European Union, beaten only by France and Denmark.[18] Not
everyone will be comforted by the fact that only about seven per
cent of live births are registered in the mother's name alone: the
proportion of officially fatherless children has risen only a little
during this time.[19] The father's identity is often well enough

[15] *Social Trends 25* (1995), Table 2.21: Fertility rates: E.C. comparison, 1970 and 1992.
[16] *Social Trends 26* (1996), Table 1.11.
[17] *Social Trends 26* (1996), Chart 2.25.
[18] *Social Trends 25* (1995), Chart 2.27: Live births outside marriage: E.C. comparison,
1992. This was before the recent enlargement.
[19] *Social Trends 24* (1994), Chart 2.21: this does not reveal what impact, if any, the
Child Support Act 1991 may have upon the willingness of either parent to name
the father at registration.

Live births outside marriage as a percentage of all births

2.25

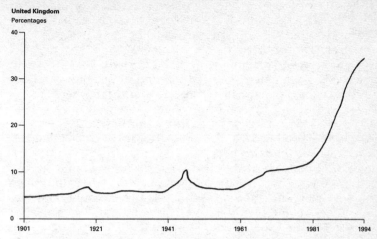

United Kingdom
Percentages

Source: Social Trends 26 (1996). Crown copyright 1996 Reproduced by permission of the Controller of HMSO and the Office for National Statistics

2.21 Live births outside marriage as a percentage of all births: by registration

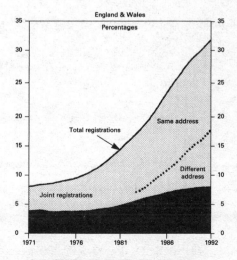

Source: Social Trends 24 (1994). Crown copyright 1994 Reproduced by permission of the Controller of HMSO and the Office for National Statistics

known in many cases, but these fatherless children have always been seen as a social problem, although a manageable one: "the bastard, like the prostitute, thief, and beggar, belongs to hat motley crowd of disreputable social types which society has generally resented, always endured."[20]

The more recent phenomenon is the growth in two-parent families where the parents are not married to one another. Both parents are named in more than three-quarters of registered births outside marriage in England and Wales and well over half of these give the same address.[21] For many, this will be a prelude to marriage,[22] but by no means all. Public attitudes have also changed a great deal over the same period.

In 1988, 72 per cent of men and 69 per cent of women agreed that "people who want children ought to get married"; but there was a noticeable difference of opinion between young and old, with younger people evenly split on this point.[23] It is thought that this is not just the usual generation gap: real changes are taking place in long term attitudes.[24] Most people would still prefer to get married before they become parents, but less and less is this being taken for granted. "If attitudes translate into behaviour, and this is by no means axiomatic, then these data would seem to suggest that extra-marital childbearing is not likely to diminish in the near future."[25]

It seems that many of these parents are consciously rejecting the approved legal and social framework within which to have and raise children.[26] Preliminary studies suggest that they are also more likely to separate before their children grow up than are married couples,[27] thus contributing disproportionately to the rise in lone parent families.

---

[20] K. Davis, "Illegitimacy and the Social Structure" (1939) 45 *American Journal of Sociology* 215, at p. 215.
[21] *Social Trends 24* (1994), Chart 2.21.
[22] See further on p. 47, below.
[23] J. Scott, M. Braun and D. Alwin, "The family way", in R. Jowell *et al*, *International Social Attitudes, 10th BSA report* (1993, SCPR), at p. 29.
[24] H. Wilkinson and G. Mulgan, *Freedom's Children—Work, relationships and politics for 18–34 year olds in Britain today* (1995, Demos).
[25] K.E. Kiernan and V. Estaugh, *Cohabitation: Extra-marital childbearing and social policy*, Occasional Paper 17, Family Policy Studies Centre, 1993.
[26] S. McRae, *Cohabiting Mothers* (1993, Policy Studies Institute).
[27] N. Buck *et al.*, *Changing Households: The British Household Panel Survey 1990–1992*, (1994); but see "Wrangle over cohabitation figures", *The Guardian*, December 1, 1995, p. 3.

2.11

Families headed by lone parents as a percentage[1] of all families with dependent children

Great Britain
Percentages

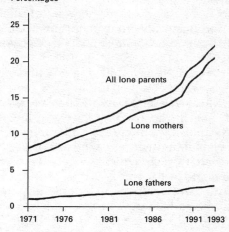

1 *Three year moving averages used (apart from 1993)*
Source: Social Trends 25 (1995). Crown copyright 1995
Reproduced by permission of the Controller of HMSO
and the Office for National Statistics

This is not all. Our teenage pregnancy rate is far and away the highest in the European Union.[28] It did fall sharply in the 1970s, but rose again the 1980s, and a more recent fall may not be sustained. Whereas 20 years ago, one-third of these pregnancies would have led to a "shotgun marriage", now less than one-tenth do so. Such marriages have declined sharply in all age groups. This again contributes to the rise in lone parent families. Also, just as birth rates vary between different ethnic groups, so too does lone parenthood; for example, more than half of mothers in the West Indian ethnic group were lone parents in 1989 to 1991.[29]

The proportion of families with dependent children headed by a lone parent more than doubled between 1971 and 1991. But we

[28] *Social Trends 25* (1995), Table 2.21.
[29] *Social Trends 24* (1994), Chart 2.9.

have already seen that the great majority of children begin life with two identified parents living at the same address. In 1991, more than three-quarters of all dependent children were still living with both their natural parents. But 16.6 per cent were living in lone parent families and most of the rest in step-families.[30] Lone parent status comes in many different forms and for short or long periods. It has been estimated that as many as one-third of all children will spend some time in a lone parent family.[31] Among other disadvantages,[32] nearly three-quarters of all such families receive income support.[33] Benefit expenditure upon families of all kinds has risen, but proportionately much more upon lone parent families.[34]

It is now much easier to avoid having unwanted children than it used to be. It would be interesting to know whether there are now more parents, whether married, cohabiting, "together but apart", or quite apart, who are consciously willing embark upon having children knowing or expecting that they will not be able to support those children without the help of public funds and services (apart from the help which is available to everyone, such as free education and health care).

It *is* clear that more parents are willing to part, despite the financial disincentives, including increased dependence on public funds. Many lone parents say that it was their choice to end their most recent relationship. However, "it does not appear that becoming a lone parent is a 'decision' taken easily, lightly or wantonly".[35] Single, non-cohabiting mothers appeared to have had the least choice. While few lone parents regretted the separation, many did not want to remain alone indefinitely or to stay on income support throughout their children's childhood. Lone parents are not, of course, sole parents. There are always two parents and usually nowadays they are both known. Even so, maintenance from the other parent has never played a large part in the finances of lone parents.[36] It is still too early to say how

---

[30] *Social Trends 25* (1995), Table 2.10.
[31] L. Clarke, *Children's changing circumstances: recent trends and future prospects* (1989, University of London, Centre for Population Studies).
[32] See p. 50, below.
[33] J. Bradshaw and J. Millar, *Lone Parent Families in the UK* (1991) Department of Social Security Research Report No. 6.
[34] *Social Trends 25* (1995), Table 8.28.
[35] Bradshaw and Millar, *op. cit.*, p. 10.
[36] *ibid.*, Chap. 7.

successful the Child Support Act 1991 will be in its long term aim of changing all this.

It should be comforting that fewer children (in absolute terms) are being looked after by local authorities or placed on child protection registers: but this could be explained as much by legal and policy changes following the Children Act 1989 as by any real increase in "good enough" parenting.

Alongside these social trends, however, are the scientific and other developments which increase the range of choices available in other ways. In the olden days, one could only choose what sort of child to have by choosing a mate; this itself could only be done within quite narrowly-defined limits and in a controlled framework.

Nowadays, it is theoretically possible to choose the genetic material from which to have a child, and by doing so to try to influence the child's own characteristics. With some, such as race, this can be by choosing sperm or eggs from a particular person: a white woman, for example, could decide to have a child by a black man. Precise characteristics are not determined until the individual child is conceived, although some techniques may increase the likelihood, for example of having a child of the desired sex. But some of those characteristics are detectable during gestation, while it is still possible to end the pregnancy. The true "designer baby" is still a long way off; but it must be the ultimate choice that the consumer society could hope to offer.

The new reproductive techniques offer social as well as genetic choices: the so-called "virgin birth" to women who have never had sexual intercourse, or at least not with the father of their child; social and genetic parenthood within lesbian relationships; childbearing after the menopause; child-producing after the death of one or both of the genetic parents; the list may not be endless but its end is not yet known.

Some of the same social results can be produced by fostering or adoption, which have been available for centuries and raise some of the same issues. The processes are, however, very different for the people concerned: having a child, even if not of one's own genetic material or conceived by the usual means, is not the same as adopting one. The range of choice is further widened by the practice of surrogacy, a half-way house between adoption and assisted reproduction.

The fact that the field of choice has been widened in all these ways does not mean that everyone is aware of what is available or is able to make a completely free choice between the options. But it does lend added force to the questions asked earlier: how far anyone is, can and should be allowed by law to make those choices and how far the suppliers of the relevant goods and services should be free to make them available to all who want them.

It is now high time to turn to the law.

CHILDBEARING INSIDE MARRIAGE

According to anthropologist Lucy Mair, "it is an ideal in all known human societies that the begetting of children should be formally licensed in some way."[37] Our way was called marriage.

This was not exactly a way of licensing individuals to have children, rather a way of regulating the framework within which they did so. Specifically, it was a way of linking the father to his children: the law recognised the link between father and mother, and having done that it presumed that all the children she bore were factually and legally his.

This was a convenient way to prove paternity. As Lord Simon of Glaisdale pointed out in *The Ampthill Peerage Case*:[38] "motherhood, although also a legal relationship, is based on a fact, being proved demonstrably by parturition. Fatherhood, by contrast, is a presumption." Since then, the science and practice of embryo transfer has proved him wrong about motherhood, just as blood tests and DNA profiling have removed the necessity for such presumptions about fatherhood. But this was the explanation for the presumption of legitimacy, which in turn was the explanation for other rules, including the double standard in the treatment of adultery.

It was also a convenient way of choosing which children to recognise as his. He and his family could select a suitable mate. She and her children would become recognised members of his family. Any others he might have were irrelevant. The mother and her family could also select a suitable mate, but she did not have the same choice in the matter of her children.

It was always a pretty crude mechanism for this purpose. Fertility as such has never been a requirement for a valid marriage. Neither has suitability either as a spouse or as a parent. The only

[37] Lucy Mair, *Marriage* (1971, Penguin Books), p. 11.
[38] [1977] A.C. 547, at p. 577D–E.

Hatchings

qualitative requirement is not to be so mentally disordered as to be unfitted for marriage.[39] Like all the other qualitative requirements, if the couple themselves do not mind, no-one else can complain.[40]

But other rules of marriage used to expect the couple to have children if they could. When the law regarded exclusion from marriage as a punishment for misbehaviour, courts were sympathetic to wives who wished to have children[41] but much less sympathetic to those who did not. They might excuse wives who had good medical reasons for avoiding childbirth, and even those who were afraid of it,[42] but not those who wished to avoid it for other reasons.[43] People the courts thought blameworthy in this respect might find themselves divorced or separated against their will, with consequences which some at least would find punitive. But such ideas of matrimonial fault lost most of their importance long before the Family Law Act 1996 was even thought of.[44]

Until remarkably recently the law had a more direct way of promoting childbearing within marriage. This was the husband's immunity from criminal liability for rape. The wife had a duty to submit to her husband's sexual requirements. More importantly, the husband could use self-help to enforce this duty. He might be punished for an assault committed in the process, but not for the rape itself.[45] The case law was sparse because husbands were not prosecuted. There is nothing to suggest that a wife could resist if she did not want to conceive or even if it would be dangerous for her to do so. This aspect of the matter was not much discussed in the debates which raged about the marital rape immunity. There were many other reasons for holding it abhorrent.[46] The judges

[39] Matrimonial Causes Act 1973, s. 12(d); first introduced in 1937.
[40] At least, that always used to be the law; the Matrimonial Causes Act 1973, s. 12, does not expressly say that only the parties to the marriage may petition, although s. 13 is clearly drafted on this basis. Recently, a father's attempt to annul the marriage of a Down's syndrome couple was abandoned, once it was clear that they both knew what they were doing: "Hugs as Down's couple win fight to stay married" *Daily Telegraph*, August 1, 1995.
[41] *White v. White* [1848] P. 330; *Walsham v. Walsham* [1949] P. 350; *Cackett v. Cackett* [1950] P. 253; *Lawrence v. Lawrence* [1950] P. 84; *Knott v. Knott* [1955] P. 249.
[42] *Fowler v. Fowler* [1952] T.L.R. 143.
[43] *Forbes v. Forbes* [1956] P. 16.
[44] See further pp. 56 *et seq*, below.
[45] *R. v. Miller* [1954] 2 Q.B. 282.
[46] Set out, *e.g.*, in Law Commission Working Paper No. 116, *Rape within Marriage*, 1990.

17

were eventually persuaded to abolish the immunity without recourse to Parliament.[47]

By 1988, the survey of British Social Attitudes[48] found that although a clear majority still thought that people who want children should get married, only one-fifth thought that the main purpose of marriage was to have children. Less than half agreed that a marriage without children is not fully complete; there was a striking difference between the generations and some between the sexes; perhaps surprisingly, women of all ages were less likely to think this than men.

To sum up, therefore, marriage used to be our method of licensing people to have children. It was always very crude. It was left to the couple and their families to assess their suitability for this purpose. The object was not to ensure that only good and suitable parents would have children. Rather it was to secure a particular familial structure for them. This was as much for the benefit of the parents, and specifically the father, as it was for the children. In particular, it allowed the father to choose which of his children he would recognise as his and for which he would accept full responsibility.

CHILDBEARING OUTSIDE MARRIAGE

Even so, it used to be thought right to deter people from having children outside marriage. There were two kinds of legal deterrent. The common law's approach was to exclude the child from the family and social structure:

> "The incapacity of a bastard consists principally in this, that he cannot be heir to anyone, neither can he have heirs, but of his own body; for being *nullius filius*, he is therefore of kin to nobody and has not ancestor from whom any heritable blood can be derived."[49]

Their exclusion from family and kin meant that they could be ignored by those who mattered. They had no claim to succeed to family property, status or power. The common law, having ignored

[47] *R. v. R.* [1992] 1 A.C. 599; supported by the European Court of Human Rights, see p. 58 below. The Law Commission nevertheless proposed legislation: Law Com. No. 205, *Rape within Marriage*, 1992. See now Sexual Offences Act 1956, s. 1, as substituted by Criminal Justice and Public Order Act 1994, s. 142.
[48] *Op. cit.*, n. 23.
[49] W. Blackstone, *Commentaries on the Laws of England*, (1st ed., 1765), Book 1, p. 447.

the children, did not feel the need to impose direct penalties upon the parents.

Indeed, arguably the common law's approach was not a deterrent at all. Penalties were imposed both by ecclesiastical law and by the poor law authorities. The local justices could punish both the mother and the father and impose liabilities upon them so as to prevent the child becoming a charge upon the parish. Direct sanctions of this sort were formally abandoned in the 19th century, although the new poor law was still designed to have a deterrent effect upon those who needed its support.[50]

Once direct sanctions against the parents had gone, discrimination against the child became increasingly unacceptable. Blackstone had acknowledged that "really any other distinction, but that of not inheriting, which civil policy renders necessary, would, with regard to the innocent offspring of his parents' crimes, be odious, unjust, and cruel to the last degree."[51] In this century, the distinction of not inheriting has seemed less and less necessary. This is only partly because of the decline in the comparative importance of inherited property as against other resources. Ideas and feelings also matter.

The common law may have found it easier to reach this conclusion than some other legal systems. There has always been a strong emphasis on allowing people to leave their property as they wish. If property is to be tied up for any length of time it must be through a tailor-made settlement which can nominate or describe the people who will qualify to succeed. Although we do now allow family members to ask for more if the will or the rules of intestate succession do not make proper provision for them,[52] there are no automatic and unbreakable rights based upon family relationship. These children could always be left property expressly. So it was easy to begin by allowing them rights of intestate succession from the mother[53] and then from the father.[54] By the same token, they could always be disinherited by will. It

[50] H. Elisofon, "A Historical and Comparative Study of Bastardy" (1973) 2 Anglo-Am. L.R. 306.
[51] *Op. cit.*
[52] Inheritance (Provision for Family and Dependants) Act 1975, replacing powers first enacted in the Inheritance (Family Provision) Act 1938.
[53] Legitimacy Act 1926, s. 9 (since repealed and replaced by the Family Law Reform Act 1969, itself repealed and replaced by the Family Law Reform Act 1987).
[54] Family Law Reform Act 1969, s. 14 (since repealed and replaced by the Family Law Reform Act 1987).

was more difficult to extend the same policy to all relationships: other donors might not think, or might not like, to provide expressly for the exclusion of relationships traced outside marriage.

In the end, however, the law decided to do away with the concept altogether.[55] Section 1(1) of the Family Law Reform Act 1987 provides that, in future:

"... references (however expressed) to any relationship between two persons shall, unless the contrary intention appears, be construed without regard to whether or not the father and mother of either of them, or the father and mother of any person through whom the relationship is deduced, have or had been married to each other at any time."

Only a common lawyer steeped in the English tradition of legislative drafting could regard that as a "ringing declaration"of the rights of people born outside wedlock, but that is just what it is. It does away with the exclusion from membership of the whole family which was their main disability. The 1987 Act also provided that the financial obligations of parents to support their children were the same whatever the circumstances of their birth.[56] The only remaining discrimination between the children lies in the right to inherit titles and other honours or their father's United Kingdom citizenship.[57]

Both England and Scotland have done their best to rid themselves of the language as well as the law of legitimacy and illegitimacy. The English originally suggested using the terms "marital" and "non-marital" to describe the children of parents who were not married to one another. The Scots led the way in denouncing the use of any discriminatory adjectives applying to the child.[58] They thought it unnecessary to bring in new labels, which would "rapidly take an old connotations". The English redrafted their proposals accordingly.[59]

The most recent and conclusive demonstration of this policy of

[55] Family Law Reform Act 1987; Law Com. No. 118, *Illegitimacy*, 1982; Law Com. No. 157, *Illegitimacy (Second Report)*, 1986.
[56] See now Children Act 1989, s. 15 and Sched. 1.
[57] British Nationality Act 1981, s. 50(9)(b).
[58] Scot Law Com. No. 82, *Report on Illegitimacy*, 1984; Law Reform (Parent and Child) (Scotland) Act 1986.
[59] Law Com. No. 157, 1986.

non-discrimination is in the Human Fertilisation and Embryology Act 1990. The 1987 Act had already provided that the husband of a woman who had a child by donor insemination would usually become the child's father for all legal purposes; the 1990 Act extended something like this to her unmarried partner.[60]

The object was to do away with discrimination against the child. Anything less is likely to fall foul of his "right to respect for his private and family life", guaranteed by Article 8 of the European Convention on Human Rights.[61] Once the child has been born, his family life must be respected. Setting restrictions on the recognition of the child's relationship with the mother and the mother's parents contravened this article.[62] Indeed, the very fact of birth creates family ties between a child and both his parents; the State must then act in a manner "calculated to enable that tie to be developed and legal safeguards must be created that render possible as from the moment of birth the child's integration in his family".[63]

This does not mean that the parents' status must be identical, provided that it is possible to recognise the father's relationship with the child. English law does this automatically, once the fact of paternity is shown, for the purposes of succession and financial provision for the child. The Child Support Act 1991 has strengthened the financial responsibilities of all parents. But an unmarried father does not have automatic "parental responsibility" for his child's upbringing.[64] He can, however, acquire this very easily, either by agreement with the mother or by court order.[65] The courts regard it as a good thing for a child to have two parents with responsibility for his upbringing: an order is likely to be granted to any father who has some relationship with and commitment to his child, even if he is not able to do much about it at the time.[66] Some people seem to think that the

---

[60] See p. 28, below.
[61] See p. 8, above.
[62] *Marckx v. Belgium* (1979) Series A No. 31; 2 E.H.R.R. 330.
[63] *Keegan v. Ireland* (1994) Series A No. 290; 18 E.H.R.R. 342, para. 50; *Kroon v. The Netherlands* (1994) Series A No. 297-C; 19 E.H.R.R. 263, para. 32; see also *Rasmussen v. Denmark* (1984) Series A No. 87; 7 E.H.R.R. 371; *Johnston v. Ireland* (1986) Series A No. 112; 9 E.H.R.R. 203;
[64] Children Act 1989, s. 2(2).
[65] *ibid.*, s. 4; as to orders, repeating provision first made in the Family Law Reform Act 1987, s. 4.
[66] The leading case is probably *Re H. (Minors) (Local Authority: Parental Rights) No. 3)* [1991] Fam. 151, C.A.; see further p. 75, below.

courts are less likely to recognise the benefits to a child of developing a positive relationship with his father, through contact and parental responsibility orders, than they would be if the parents were married to one another; but this is not borne out by the decided cases.

The old stereotype was of an unmarried mother desperate to blame a man of substance for her situation, so that she could squeeze a little maintenance from him. Her word was not to be trusted without corroboration. This too was abolished in 1987. These days it is just as likely that the father will be wanting to establish his link with the child. There is still a presumption that a child born to a married woman is her husband's child: neither of them has to prove it. But it can easily be disproved.[67] On the other hand, it has been said that fatherhood itself must be proved to a standard commensurate with its seriousness.[68] But DNA testing makes it provable to a much higher standard than that. This means that it is no longer possible, either in fact or in law, for a father to pick and choose which of his children to recognise as his. He must now accept some responsibility for all of them, as the mother has always had to do.

Thus while marriage is still available, and the framework preferred by most people who want to have children, the law does not insist upon or even directly encourage it. The law contains very few reasons for men or women to have children only within marriage; rather, as we shall see in the next chapter, there are still good reasons for the parent who is going to do most of the work of looking after the children to do this within marriage; but that is a different issue.

The most dramatic changes in the law have taken place in the last quarter century.[69] They coincide almost exactly with the steep rise in births outside marriage. They also coincide with the changes in public attitudes. Now is not the time to enter into the "which comes first" argument. Anyone who would like the law to go back to what it used to be would have to get over, not only the changes in public attitudes, but also the very simple arguments which led to the 1969 reforms:

---

[67] The Family Law Reform Act 1969, in s. 26, provides that the presumption of legitimacy may be rebutted on the balance of probabilities; and in ss. 20 to 25 for blood tests to determine paternity.

[68] *Re JS* [1981] Fam. 22; *W. v. K (Proof of Paternity)* [1988] 1 F.L.R. 86.

[69] The Family Law Reform Act 1969; the Family Law Reform Act 1987; the Children Act 1989; and the Human Fertilisation and Embryology Act 1990.

"At the root of any suggestion for the improvement of the lot of bastards ... is, of course, that in one sense they start level with legitimate children, in that no child is created of his own volition. Whatever may be said of the parents, the bastard is innocent of any wrong-doing. To allow to him an inferior, or indeed unrecognised, status ... is to punish him for a wrong of which he was not guilty."[70]

NO CHILDBEARING AT ALL

If marriage is no longer used for this purpose, what other methods of control could there be? The tone of some of the press comments about "Sarah" came close to suggesting that some people should be forcibly prevented from having children.

It is not absolutely unlawful to deprive a person of his powers of reproduction. In once case,[71] Lord Denning took the view that sterilisation, at least without a very good reason, fell within the category of acts so intrinsically harmful as to be unlawful irrespective of consent;[72] but the other judges disagreed. A person is now free voluntarily to surrender or limit his or her own fertility.[73]

But what about involuntary interventions? These too are not absolutely unlawful. That argument was rejected by the House of Lords in *Re B (A Minor) (Wardship: Sterilisation)*:[74] the court may consent to the sterilisation of a child. In another context altogether, the Court of Appeal has even said that the court may consent to an operation in the face of objections from a child who is capable of making the decision for herself.[75] It seems unlikely, to say the least, that they would extend this principle to a permanent sterilisation, although it is not impossible.

Where children are involved, the criterion is undoubtedly what is in their own best interests. It is difficult to see how it could ever be in the best interests of a child of sufficient age and understanding to sterilise her against her will solely for

---

[70] *Report of the Committee on the Law of Succession in relation to Illegitimate Persons,* Chairman: The Rt. Hon. Lord Justice Russell, Cmnd. 3051, 1966, para. 19.
[71] *Bravery v. Bravery* [1954] 3 All E.R. 59.
[72] See further on p. 96, below.
[73] In one situation, it is thought that the pressures upon him to do so may be so great that extra safeguards are required: under the Mental Health Act 1983, s. 57, an independent assessment of the patient's capacity to consent is required for the surgical implantation of hormones to reduce male sexual drive.
[74] [1988] A.C. 199.
[75] *Re W (A Minor) (Medical Treatment: Court's Jurisdiction)* [1993] Fam. 64.

contraceptive or menstrual management purposes. But it might be different if her life or health were permanently threatened by a disease, the only cure for which would result in permanent infertility.

If an adult is unable to make the decision for herself, no-one else has the right to consent on her behalf. But the House of Lords in *Re F (Mental Patient: Sterilisation)*[76] reached much the same result by a different route. Where a person is permanently incapable of taking the decision in question, it is lawful for other people to do whatever is necessary in that person's own best interests. Usually there is no need to go to court. But the court can grant a declaration that a proposed course of action is (or is not) lawful in the circumstances. As a matter of practice, said the House of Lords, a declaration should be sought in sensitive cases like these. They were fully aware of the risk that decisions might otherwise be made by people who were too close to the problem to take a properly objective view of the seriousness of what they were doing,[77] that operations might be carried out for the convenience of carers or even for administrative convenience, let alone for more sinister purposes. The need to seek the approval of the court is some protection for everyone concerned.

Since then, however, sterilisations for purely therapeutic reasons, and even for menstrual management, have been excluded from this safeguard.[78] Presumably, compulsory male sterilisation for purely contraceptive purposes is subject to the same legal requirements as female; but it seems that the question has not yet reached the courts, perhaps because it is never done, or because it has never occurred to anyone to look at it in the same light.

In the event, therefore, it is likely that most proposed operations which will have the effect of sterilising an adult do not in fact find their way to the courts. In practice, this may be no bad thing. The courts are not necessarily the right place in which to weigh the evidence and arguments in a particular case. Often these point

---

[76] [1990] 2 A.C. 1; the Scots have reached much the same conclusion but by a different route, in *L v. I's Curator ad litem*, *The Times*, March 19, 1996.

[77] As in *Re D (A Minor) (Wardship: Sterilisation)* [1976] Fam. 185.

[78] See *Re E (A Minor) (Medical Treatment)* [1991] 2 F.L.R. 585; *Re GF (Medical Treatment)* [1992] 1 F.L.R. 293; both menstrual management cases. In *Re GF*, the President of the Family Division excepted sterilisations from court approval only where two doctors were satisfied that (1) the operation was necessary for therapeutic purposes; (2) it was in the best interests of the patient; and (3) there was no practicable, less obtrusive alternative treatment.

overwhelmingly in one direction, so that there is no dispute for the court to resolve.

It is still difficult to justify the line between those which do and those which do not need court approval. There is a real difference between preventing a person ever becoming pregnant (or making another person pregnant) in the future and preventing a woman suffering from the painful or distressing effects of her present heavy menstruation. If there is no independent scrutiny, who is to know whether or not the real purpose of an operation is contraception or menstrual management? It would be relatively easy for anyone to disguise the difference, perhaps even to himself. The convenience of sterilisation for menstrual management purposes is at least as great as it is for contraception. There is also a difference in kind and in principle between removing a healthy womb for such a purpose and removing diseased tissue from any of the reproductive organs, in which the resulting infertility is truly an incidental effect.

In some common law jurisdictions, all procedures which result or are likely to result in permanent infertility require independent approval.[79] It is perhaps unlikely that this is always obtained in practice. In this country, there is quite a strong feeling that the process of submitting proposals to the court is wasteful and unnecessary. Most seem to think, however, that some safeguards are necessary. The Law Commission provisionally proposed that judicial approval should be required for all sterilisations for the purpose of either contraception or menstrual management.[80] In the eventual report, this was modified in the light of consultation with, among others, the Official Solicitor. Any treatment or procedure intended or reasonably likely to cause permanent infertility should require judicial approval, unless it is to treat a disease of the reproductive organs or to relieve the existing detrimental effects of menstruation; for the latter, however, an independent second medical opinion would be required.[81] This is principally to prevent easy avoidance of the need to go to court; interestingly, the Commission do not regard mere "discomfort or distress" as a "detrimental effect" of menstruation.

The courts may not be the best place in which to resolve these

[79] *e.g.* in South Australia and New South Wales.
[80] Law Commission Consultation Paper No. 129, *Mentally Incapacitated Adults and Decision-Making: Medical Treatment and Research*, 1993, paras. 6.2 and 6.8.
[81] Law Com. No. 231, *Mental Incapacity*, 1995, paras. 6.4, 6.9.

difficult dilemmas in individual cases. But unless and until Parliament is prepared to do so, they ought to be the best place to examine the principles involved. They have reached the position that the guiding principle is the best interests of the individual concerned. Unfortunately, some of the speeches in *Re F*[82] appear to identify this with the well-known test in *Bolam v. Friern Hospital Management Committee*[83] for deciding whether or not a doctor has been negligent: that is, whether he has acted in accordance with a responsible body of medical opinion, even if others would have acted otherwise.

This should certainly be a minimum requirement of any decision to treat and of how the treatment is carried out; but it cannot be the only test. It provides no way of resolving a dispute between two or more equally respectable medical opinions. A similar approach is used by doctors supplying second opinions for certain controversial treatments under the Mental Health Act 1983: not surprisingly, it means that certificates are given even when the second opinion doctor would not himself have treated the patient in the same way.[84]

Moreover, decisions on matters as fundamental as the loss of reproductive capacity involve a much wider range of considerations, including the patient's own values and preferences, her social situation and whether there is any other way of resolving the perceived problems. The Law Commission have proposed that everyone, carers, courts and second opinion doctors, should have to apply the same test to anything done or decided for a person unable to act for herself: this would be her own best interests (and not those of anyone else), having regard to:

(1) her own ascertainable past and present wishes and feelings and the factors she would consider if able to do so;

(2) the need to permit and encourage her to participate, or to

---

[82] [1990] 2 A.C. 1; Lord Brandon, at p. 68C–D, expressly disagreed with the Court of Appeal that this test was insufficient in such cases; Lord Bridge at p. 52E approved the test for prophylactic or therapeutic treatment but not for these cases; Lord Jauncey, at pp. 83G–84A seems to regard the "best interests" and *Bolam* tests as cumulative; it is not clear whether Lord Griffiths at p. 69G and Lord Goff at p. 78B–C regard them as cumulative or identical.

[83] [1957] 1 W.L.R. 582; [1957] 2 All E.R. 118.

[84] P. Fennell, *Treatment without Consent under Part IV of the Mental Health Act 1983* (unpublished research report); see P. Fennell, *Treatment without Consent: Law, psychiatry and the treatment of mentally disordered people since 1845* (1996, Routledge).

improve her ability to participate, as fully as possible in anything done for her;

(3) the views of other people whom it is appropriate and practicable to consult about her wishes and feelings and what would be in her best interests; and

(4) whether the purpose can be as effectively achieved in way which is less restrictive of her freedom of action.[85]

All of this assumes that the person is unable to decide for herself. The dividing line for compulsory sterilisation is not between those who are, or are not, capable of bearing or rearing children. Rather, it is between those who are, or are not, capable of making the decision for themselves. The courts have so far devoted little attention to the precise test of incapacity for this purpose; the reported cases have all concerned women with severe mental disability. The usual test of capacity in English law is whether or not the person is capable of understanding in broad terms the nature and effects of what is proposed. Yet being pregnant and having a baby, and going to sleep while something is done to your tummy which will prevent this, are not in themselves particularly difficult concepts to understand.

The "broad terms" test was expressly rejected and something more precise defined in *Re C (Refusal of Medical Treatment).*[86] This concerned a Broadmoor patient who successfully objected to having a below knee amputation for a potentially fatal gangrenous foot. Mr Justice Thorpe held that, to be capable of deciding for himself, the patient had (1) to comprehend and retain relevant information; (2) to believe it; and (3) to weigh it in the balance to arrive at a choice.

This is similar, but not identical, to the approach proposed by the Law Commission.[87] A person would be without the capacity to decide for herself if she suffered from a "mental disability" which resulted in either or two conditions. The first would cover someone who is unable to understand or retain the information relevant to the decision, including information about the consequences of making and failing to make it; but it would not cover someone who can understand an explanation of this information "given in broad terms and simple language". The

---

[85] Law Com. No. 231, paras. 3.24–3.27.
[86] [1994] 1 W.L.R. 290; [1994] 1 All E.R. 819.
[87] Law Com. No. 231, paras. 3.3–3.19.

second would cover someone who can understand the relevant information, but is unable because of her mental disability to make a decision based upon it; this might include someone whose delusions prevented her from believing the information she was given; or whose compulsions meant that she could not use it; or whose learning disabilities made her unable to resist the influence of others. The test would not cover someone simply because she had made a decision which would not be made by "a person of ordinary prudence".

It is all too easy for well-meaning people to believe that they are acting for the best if they prevent a disabled person from having children. But if we reject the idea of licensing parents in advance, it is essential to hold onto two fundamental principles: first, that compulsion can only be used upon people who are unable to decide and not upon people who are unable to be good parents; and secondly, that any decision taken on their behalf must be taken in their own best interests and not for the sake of others.

CHOOSING WHAT CHILDREN TO HAVE

All of the above assumes that the parents are able or want to have children by conventional means. Many, perhaps as many as one in six couples, have difficulty in doing so.[88] Others may choose not to do so. Infertility and childlessness are different things.[89] Some people may be physically capable of having children in the usual way, but for a variety of reasons (sexual, social, medical or genetic) may want or need to have a child in an unusual way. Both the infertile and the childless may then look for help from others.

There are now several sources of supply—adoption or fostering, assisted reproduction, and surrogacy. All of these are regulated by the law to a certain extent. They offer an opportunity for vetting procedures which does not exist with ordinary reproduction. But they also give the would-be parents a much greater opportunity to choose the sort of children they want to have. The implications of this are much more frightening than anything presented by the "Sarahs".

[88] Human Fertilisation and Embryology Authority, *The Patients' Guide to DI and IVF Clinics* (1995), p. 4; the source is probably M. Hull *et al*, "Population study of causes, treatment and outcome of infertility" (1985) 291 B.M.J. 1693.
[89] G. Douglas, "Assisted Reproduction and the Welfare of the Child" (1993) 46 (II) C.L.P. 10.

By Michael Heath

ADOPTION AND FOSTERING

The earliest solution was adoption. When families were all about lineage and succession, legal systems based on Roman law recognised adoption as a means of transferring a person, not necessarily a child, from one family to another. The common law did not. Then families became more child-centred, and wanted both to have a child to look after and to give a home to a child who needed one. Even so, the common lawyers had some difficulty seeing the point of turning this from a *de facto* into a legal situation.[90] They proceeded with caution. But their caution was

[90] *Report of the Committee on Child Adoption*, Chairman: Sir Alfred Hopkinson K.C.,

about disturbing the laws of succession rather than about vetting the proposed adopters.

However, from the first it was taken for granted that paying money in direct exchange for a child was wrong. This is still an offence.[91] In theory, the court then cannot grant an adoption order,[92] but there is a curious provision saying that it is not an offence at all if retrospectively authorised by the court which makes the order.[93]

The trend of the law since the first Adoption of Children Act 1926 has been towards greater and greater legal integration of the child into the adoptive family.[94] At the same time there has also been greater and greater control over the process of selection and placement. First, the adoption agencies were placed under regulation.[95] Then, almost all direct and private placements were forbidden.[96] The processes of selecting children for adoption, parents to adopt, and making the link between the two, are all subject to detailed statutory regulation,[97] under the ultimate supervision of the court to which the agency must make a detailed report;[98] and in difficult cases there will also be a guardian *ad litem* to protect the interests of the child.

All of this is designed to ensure that only those whose suitability has been carefully assessed are allowed to adopt. Adoption remains an exception to the general removal of distinctions between married and unmarried parenthood. Only married couples may adopt jointly,[99] although an unmarried or permanently separated person may adopt alone.[1] In practice, unmarried couples may be allowed to adopt in this way, but it will mean that the child only has one half of the usual family

Cmd. 1254, 1921; *Report (first) of the Child Adoption Committee*, Chairman: Mr Justice Tomlin, Cmd. 2401, 1925.
[91] Adoption Act 1976, s. 57(2).
[92] *ibid.*, s. 24(2).
[93] *ibid.*, s. 57(3).
[94] Culminating in the Children Act 1975, which placed an adopted child in almost all respects in the same position as a child born of the adopters' marriage.
[95] Adoption of Children (Regulation) Act 1939; *Report of the Departmental Committee on Adoption Societies and Agencies*, Chairman: Miss Florence Horsburgh M.P., Cmd. 5499, 1937.
[96] Children Act 1975; *Report of the Departmental Committee on the Adoption of Children*, Chairman: Sir William Houghton, Cmnd. 5107, 1972.
[97] See Adoption Agencies Regulations 1983.
[98] Adoption Rules 1984, Sched. 2.
[99] Adoption Act 1976, s. 14(1), (1A), (1B).
[1] *ibid.*, s. 15(1).

network. The adoptive parent's partner can share parental
responsibility for bringing up the child if there is an order that the
child is to live with them both; but he or she could never be made
to contribute financially to the child's maintenance. Despite this,
neither the Adoption Law Review nor the Government has
proposed that unmarried couples should be allowed to adopt
jointly.[2]

The Government has proposed that the selection procedures
should be operated with rather more flexibility in future. There
are several good reasons for having these controls, but they are
supposed to be for the benefit of the individual children and their
families, rather than for any other purpose.

First, during its heyday, most of the research indicated that
conventional adoption was a spectacular success; but that heyday
is long gone. In 1925, it was said that there were far more children
needing new homes than there were people wanting to adopt
them. Nowadays, however, the reverse is true. There are very few
healthy white babies offered for adoption. As we are unwilling to
allow rationing by price, rigorous selection criteria are one way of
making the system workable.

Secondly, adoptive homes are now being sought for children
whose parents do not want them adopted. Often it can be said
that those parents have forfeited their own claims by the way in
which they have behaved towards their children. But this is not
always so. At least since the House of Lords' decision in *Re W (An
Infant)*,[3] it has been possible to dispense with parental agreement
on the ground that it is being unreasonably withheld, even though
she cannot be blamed for the situation which has arisen: a
reasonable parent would give greater weight to her child's
interests than to her own. It cannot be just, either to such parents
or to their children, to insist upon a transfer to a new family unless
it is virtually certain that the new family will be an improvement
upon the old.[4]

Thirdly, many of the children now being adopted have special

---

[2] *Review of Adoption Law, Report to Ministers of an Inter-Departmental Working Group*,
1992, Department of Health and Welsh Office; Department of Health and Others,
Adoption: The Future, Cm. 2288, 1993, para. 4.39.
[3] [1971] A.C. 682.
[4] The new ground for dispensing with parental agreement originally proposed
would emphasise that the advantages for the child of being transferred into a new
family should be so significantly better than those of any other option as to justify
overriding the parents' objections: Cm. 2288, *op. cit.*, para. 5.5.

needs of one sort or another; these may arise from their own characteristics or their early lives or a combination of the two. Children are being adopted at an older age, when their own relationships and life-stories have already been established. Parenting one's own children is difficult enough: special qualities are needed to be able to parent someone else's child and in such circumstances. As it is, the evidence is that our selection techniques are very far from perfect.[5]

These developments mean that adoption is less often available as a solution to infertility. For some, perhaps many, of the children who need adoptive homes today, the best prospective adopters may be people who want to add to their existing family, rather than to seek a substitute for the one they never had. For others, the best adopter may be someone who is not infertile but has for other reasons chosen to remain childless. A single person may be able to give to a child exactly the concentrated attention which his special needs demand.

But all these careful scrutiny and selection procedures have been called into question by the development of inter-country adoption. Couples have increasingly been going abroad to look for children to adopt.[6] The rigorous selection procedures which operate at home do not apply. There is no international adoption agency which can perform this role and ensure uniform standards. For a long time our professionals so disapproved of the whole idea that they were reluctant to do anything which looked like helping it. Yet in practice it could not be stopped.

In practice it also looks like a market. Those who can afford to do so are able to secure children through intermediaries whom they often pay quite handsomely, sometimes in circumstances where it is difficult to know much about the child or his family of birth. Some attempt had to be made to ensure that the children imported were not going to suffer harm or be rapidly abandoned to the authorities here like unwanted pets after Christmas.

[5] J. Thoburn, *Success and Failure in Permanent Family Placement* (1990); J. Fratter, J. Rowe and J. Thoburn, *Permanent Family Placement: a decade of experience*, (BAAF Research Series No. 8, 1991). See generally Social Services Inspectorate, *Research which has a Bearing on Adoption or Alternatives to Adoption* (1993); based particularly upon J. Thoburn, *Review of Research relating to Adoption* (Inter-Departmental Review of Adoption Law) (Background paper Number 2, 1990).
[6] Inter-Departmental Review of Adoption Law, Background Paper No. 3, *Intercountry Adoption*, 1991; Social Services Inspectorate, *Adoption of Children from Overseas*, 1991.

Some regulation has already been introduced through immigration procedures which require a welfare investigation before the child is brought into the country.[7] These home study reports are perhaps the closest we come to giving people a licence to parent. But local authorities have no express power or duty to provide them, or to charge for them, although most now do so. Inevitably, this contributes to the impression that those with the funds to do so are effectively able to buy themselves a baby.

The Government's view is that "the wishes of parents [*sic*] here who want to adopt a child from overseas should be respected and in all suitable cases supported and facilitated".[8] At the same time, so far as is realistic, it wants the same principles and safeguards as there are in domestic adoption. Apart from the financial considerations, however, the major difference is that in domestic adoptions we can start with the child and go looking for the right parents for him. Inter-country adoptions start with the parents who go looking for the right child for them. Provided that they are willing to look abroad, and have the resources to do so, they are more likely to be able to select the child of their choice than they would be if they stayed at home.

ASSISTED REPRODUCTION

Assisted reproduction is another solution, not only to infertility but also to childlessness. In all its forms, more would-be parents are probably helped in this way than by adoption.[9] Legally, it is a complex and confusing topic. Many of the treatments available for infertility are not subject to any form of legal regulation other than that involved in all medical practice. Would-be parents can obtain them either through the NHS or privately without any special selection processes, apart from those involved in their local health authorities' policies and the clinical judgment of the doctors treating them. These methods include the use of drugs to stimulate

[7] Inter-departmental Review of Adoption Law, Consultation Paper No. 4, *Intercountry Adoption*, 1992.
[8] Cm. 2288, *op. cit.*, para. 6.10.
[9] There were just over 3,000 live births following IVF and 1,500 following donor insemination in the United Kingdom in 1993; see Human Fertilisation and Embryology Authority, Fourth Annual Report, 1995, p. 29. Excluding step-parent adoptions, only about 3,500 children are adopted in England and Wales each year, and in 1991, only 900 of these were babies adopted soon after birth; see Cm. 2288, *op. cit.*, paras. 3.3, 3.9.

ovulation, which may well result in multiple pregnancies with all their attendant physical, social and moral problems. For most purposes, they also include placing the couple's own eggs and sperm into the woman, known as gamete intrafallopian transfer (GIFT), which from the couple's point of view must seem little different from fertilising the egg outside the body and replacing the resultant embryo.

Two types of treatment, however, can only be given under the terms of a licence granted by the Human Fertilisation and Embryology Authority (HFEA). The first is any form of treatment which involves donated gametes—that is, where a woman is inseminated with sperm from someone other than her regular partner, or where a woman is treated using eggs from another woman.[10] The second is any form of treatment involving the creation of an embryo outside the body,[11] known as in vitro fertilisation (IVF). Sometimes, both are involved, where donated eggs and/or sperm are used in IVF.

There were different reasons for singling out these particular procedures for special treatment in the law.[12] Donating sperm is quite straightforward, as is using it for artificial insemination. Certain safeguards and standards may be essential but the same is true of many medical and obstetric procedures. Donating eggs is not so straightforward, nor are the procedures for using them in treatment, but that is not what brings them into a special category. Special treatment is justified by the fact of donation, introducing different genetic material into the usual processes of conception and childbirth.

IVF raises other considerations. Even if the couple's own gametes are used, the procedure is likely to produce "spare" embryos which cannot immediately be used. They will therefore have to be allowed to perish, used for immediate research, or stored for possible future use either in treatment or research. Such potential human beings deserve the special protection of the law. For similar reasons, the storage of gametes also requires a licence.[13] Although at the time only sperm and embryos could successfully

[10] Human Fertilisation and Embryology Act 1990, s. 4(1)(b).
[11] *ibid.*, ss. 3(1)(a) and 1(2).
[12] These arguments are implicit rather than explicit in the discussion of whether or not these practices should be allowed at all, in the *Report of the Committee of Inquiry into Human Fertilisation and Embryology*, Chairman: Dame Mary Warnock DBE, Cmnd. 9314, 1984, Chaps. 4–7.
[13] 1990 Act, s. 4(1)(a).

be frozen for future use, work was also proceeding on effective methods of freezing eggs.

Whatever the original reasons for singling out these two types of treatment, people who want them must go to clinics which meet the quality and other criteria contained in the Human Fertilisation and Embryology Act 1990 and the HFEA's Code of Practice.[14]

The Act also insists that "a woman shall not be provided with treatment services unless account has been taken of the welfare of any child who may be born as a result of the treatment (including the need of that child for a father), and of any other child who may be affected by the birth".[15] Confusingly, this provision applies to any treatment services,[16] whether or not they need a licence, but it operates as a condition of a licence and therefore only applies to licensed centres. It was introduced during the passage of the bill through Parliament, in response to pressure to limit treatment to married couples.[17] It is extremely difficult to work out just what it is trying to achieve and how to do this.

Some of the precautions required in the HFEA Code of Practice would be regarded as good practice in any event. Centres must take all reasonable steps to ensure that people receiving treatment and any children resulting from it have the best possible protection from harm to their health.[18] For example, gamete donors should be screened for HIV and other infections which might be passed on to mother or child.[19] Eggs, sperm and embryos should not be used if they have been subject to procedures which may harm their developmental potential,[20] or exposed to contamination.[21] Care should be taken in carrying out the procedures themselves, some of which require considerable skill, for example in manipulating egg and sperm under a microscope. Failure to meet these standards might well result in liability under ordinary contractual or tortious principles, at least towards the couple

---

[14] Human Fertilisation and Embryology Authority, Code of Practice, Second Revision, December 1995.

[15] 1990 Act, s. 13(5).

[16] Defined in the 1990 Act, s. 2(1) as medical, surgical or obstetric services provided to the public or a section of the public for the purpose of assisting women to carry children.

[17] See the account in D. Morgan and R. Lee, *Blackstone's Guide to the Human Fertilisation and Embryology Act 1990*, pp. 142–4.

[18] Code, para. 3.1.

[19] *ibid.*, paras. 3.2, 3.33, 3.46 to 3.50.

[20] *ibid.*, paras. 7.5, 7.6.

[21] *ibid.*, para. 7.8.

receiving treatment, and sometimes towards the child as well.

In a rather different category is the Code's requirement that no more than three eggs or embryos be placed in a woman in any one cycle, whether by GIFT or by any other method.[22] This can certainly be said to be for the sake of the children's welfare. It will reduce the many problems for mother and children which arise from multiple pregnancy and birth. Generally speaking, the fewer the better for those who survive. But, at least in the early days, the chances of achieving a successful pregnancy were better if more eggs or embryos were replaced. There can be considerable consumer pressure upon clinics to maximise those chances whatever the problems it may cause in the end.

In yet another category are the obligations placed upon centres to make some assessment of the suitability of the prospective parents as parents. This is undoubtedly what Parliament intended by the injunction to take account of the welfare of "any resulting child". Some wanted to restrict treatment, if not to married couples, then at least to people in stable heterosexual relationships. At first, some doctors thought that this was what the Act required.

In fact, both the Act and the Code avoid such automatic judgments. No category of woman is legally excluded from treatment.[23] People seeking treatment "are entitled to a fair and unprejudiced assessment of their situation and needs".[24] However, "centres should take note in their procedures of the importance of a stable and supportive environment for any child produced as a result of treatment."[25]

For any licensed treatment, centres should bear in mind:

(a) the prospective parents' commitment to having and bringing up a child;
(b) their ability to provide a stable and supportive environment for any resulting child;
(c) their own and their families' medical histories;
(d) their ages and future likely ability to look after or provide for a child's needs;
(e) their ability to meet the needs of any resulting child, including the implications of any multiple births;

[22] *ibid.*, para. 7.9.
[23] *ibid.*, para. 3.14.
[24] *ibid.*, para. 3.16.
[25] *ibid.*, para. 3.14, this is new to the 1995 revision.

(f) any risk of harm to any resulting child, including the risk of inherited disorder, problems during pregnancy and of neglect or abuse;

(g) the effect of any new baby upon any existing child of the family.[26]

If donation is involved, centres should also take into account:

(a) a child's potential need to know his origins and whether the parents are prepared for this;
(b) the possible attitudes of other members of the family;
(c) the implications for the child if the donor is personally known within the family; and
(d) any possible dispute about legal fatherhood.[27]

Where treatment is offered to a single woman who has no male partner, the child will have no legal father. The Act and Code do not outlaw this (any more than adoption by a single woman is outlawed by the Adoption Act) but some would think it a disadvantage for a child to be legally deprived of one half of the usual network of family and kin. The State might also suffer if there is only one parent legally liable to support the child. The Code merely requires centres to consider the mother's ability to meet all the child's needs and the support systems available to help her do this.[28]

It is doubtful how rigorously these assessments are in fact conducted. An early research study concluded that the Act had made little difference to clinical practice.[29] Treatment is rarely refused on these grounds, although special care may be taken before providing treatment in some cases, particularly to single women or those in lesbian partnerships. Few practitioners would regard the situation in the same light as an adoption placement. But what reasons are there to impose any sort of assessment at all?

When donation is involved, there is at least some parallel with adoption. Genetically, the effect of sperm or egg donation is the

---

[26] *ibid.*, para. 3.17; the 1995 revision spells these matters out even more clearly than the earlier versions.
[27] *ibid.*, para. 3.18.
[28] *ibid.*, para. 3.19.a; para. 3.19.b deals with surrogacy arrangements; see p. 43, below.
[29] G. Douglas, *Access to assisted reproduction: legal and other criteria for eligibility* (1992, Cardiff Law School).

same as a step-parent adoption; if both sperm and eggs are donated, the effect is the same as a conventional adoption. Legally, however, the effect is immediate, automatic and more extreme. The Act provides that the carrying mother is always the legal mother, whatever the genetic position, and whether or not the child is intended for her or is being carried because of a surrogacy arrangement.[30] Where donated sperm is used, the mother's husband automatically becomes the child's father, unless it is shown that he did not consent to the treatment;[31] even if the couple are unmarried, the mother's partner becomes the father, provided that they are being treated together.[32] Even the limited exceptions which remain after an adoption do not apply here.[33] His parental responsibility for bringing up the child will, like that of any other father, depend upon whether or not he is married to the mother.[34]

Although the effects are similar to adoption, the process is very different. The mother carries and gives birth to the child like any other mother. Until very recently, donation was regarded as a "cure" for infertility. Secrecy and concealment were not only condoned but positively encouraged. Sperm donation is still almost always completely anonymous. Egg donation from known donors, for example between sisters, is probably more common. The HFEA now maintains a register of donors which would theoretically allow the link to be traced. But at present this is not possible and the Act prohibits a change which would apply to donations taking place before it is allowed.[35] Limited information about the donor is kept on the register and the child will eventually be able to learn something about his origins. But this cannot be compared with the right to inspect the original birth certificate which now enables many adopted children to trace their birth parents.[36] Opinions still differ about the wisdom of telling a child that he has been born of donated gametes, whereas it is taken for granted that an adopted child has the "right to know".

Some might think that these were added reasons for taking great

---

[30] 1990 Act, s. 27.
[31] 1990 Act, s. 28(2).
[32] 1990 Act, s. 28(3); this is perhaps less likely in a surrogacy arrangement; see *Re Q (Parental Order)* [1996] 1 F.L.R. 369.
[33] *i.e.* the genetic link is retained for the purposes of the law of incest and the prohibited degrees of marriage.
[34] Children Act 1989, s. 2(2); see p. 21, above.
[35] 1990 Act, s. 31(5).
[36] Adoption Act 1976, s. 51.

care to provide treatment only to people who can be expected to place their child's welfare above their own. Others place much greater priority on relieving the misery caused by infertility or unwanted childlessness. They can readily point out that this particular child would otherwise never have been born. However miserable his life, how can he complain?

Nor is the setting one in which sophisticated social judgments can usually be expected. Although the Code of Practice says that there should be a multi-disciplinary assessment taking into account the views of everyone who has been involved with the prospective parents,[37] the professional responsibility for deciding whether to treat rests with the doctor. The person most likely to be able to offer a social perspective is the centre's counsellor, but the roles of counselling and assessment are different and to some extent contradictory. There is no-one whose task it is to do the equivalent of a home study report in an adoption.

There are parallels between adoption and donation, not only because the child is not genetically their own, but also because the gametes used are a unique resource which is in limited supply. This is particularly true of donated eggs, for few women have eggs to spare or wish to go through the procedures necessary for harvesting them. Sperm donation is much more straightforward, but the screening procedures particularly for HIV, can be a strong deterrent. There are also cultural barriers in some religious or ethnic groups.

Rationing is a process with which health care professionals are familiar, so that they may be more prepared to operate selection criteria for this purpose;[38] but these are perhaps more likely to be aimed at maximising the "take-home baby" rate than at assessing the prospective parents' suitability as parents.

If is even harder to see the reasons for trying to assess the parenting abilities of a couple who are using their own gametes. The child will be theirs in every sense. They will supply the unique resources needed. Although the other resources needed, the facilities and expertise of the centre and its staff, are in short supply, this is no different from other treatments which are more readily available to those who can pay than to those who cannot.

But that in itself is a reason for taking special care in these cases. Whatever the arguments against allowing people to buy babies to

[37] Code, para. 3.28.
[38] G. Douglas, *op. cit.*, 1992.

adopt, they apply even more strongly against allowing people to buy the creation of babies who would not otherwise exist. These techniques may eventually present entirely new opportunities for picking and choosing what sort of child to have. Prospective adopters are allowed a certain amount of choice in the kind of child they will agree to take, but they are not procuring the creation of a child to their own liking.

Donation already allows a certain amount of selection in the characteristics of the resulting child. Sperm or eggs from people with particular racial, physical or even other qualities can be selected in the hope that they will combine in the desired manner. In time, IVF may present even greater opportunities. Micromanipulation techniques already mean that both the individual egg and the individual sperm can be selected. Sooner or later, it may be possible to identify the genetic characteristics of these in advance. Although not yet with us, the scientific knowledge to create the "Brave New World" is coming closer.

"As a matter of principle," said the Warnock Committee, "we do not wish to encourage the possibility of prospective parents seeking donors with specific characteristics by the use of whose semen they wish to give birth to a particular type of child."[39] Hence detailed descriptions should not be given as a basis for choice. The HFEA Code states that when selecting gametes for treatment, "centres should take into account each prospective parent's preferences in relation to the general physical characteristics of the donor".[40] It is usually assumed that parents will want these to match their own: this can lead to difficulties in supply where the feature is comparatively rare, such as blue eyes, or where there are cultural barriers to donation with the particular ethnic group. But expressing a preference "does not allow the prospective parents to choose, for social reasons alone, a donor of different ethnic origins from themselves."[41]

In similar vein, "centres should not select the sex of embryos for social reasons"[42] and "centres should not use sperm sorting techniques in sex selection."[43] Generally speaking, the HFEA have been prepared to accept that such things may be done for good medical reasons, where the woman is at risk of having a child with

[39] *Op. cit.*, para. 4.21.
[40] Code, para. 3.22.
[41] *ibid.*
[42] *ibid.*, para. 7.20.
[43] *ibid.*, para. 7.21; in any event, it appears not to work.

a life-threatening disorder; but they found that public opinion was strongly against sex selection for purely social reasons. This is perhaps a good example of something which couples may try to achieve themselves, usually unsuccessfully, but which it would be wrong to allow them to choose with professional help.

It might be thought that the deliberate creation of another human being takes all these treatments into a different category from those which merely mend or heal an existing person. Both the Act and the Code recognise that the same argument applies to treatment services which do not require a licence. If techniques develop in such a way that it becomes possible to select the sex or other characteristics of the resulting child, this might add to the case for regulation. It will certainly raise new dilemmas. The welfare of the child might not always be the best guide. What if the parents would be very well able to meet the needs of the right sort of child but would instantly reject any other?

SURROGACY

Technically, a surrogacy arrangement is one where a mother agrees before she begins to carry a child that she will hand it over to be brought up by someone else.[44] In partial surrogacy, her own egg is fertilised, either naturally or artificially, with sperm from the commissioning father. In full surrogacy, she carries an embryo created with sperm and eggs from the commissioning couple.

These arrangements provoke strong feelings and a variety of responses from the common law legal systems. Some have tried to ban them altogether, although in practice it is hard to see how a ban on partial surrogacy could be enforced. Others have tolerated altruistic surrogacy but banned commercial arrangements, because these are seen as buying and selling a baby. But it has been known for a court to hold that the commissioning parents as the "real" parents and deny the surrogate mother any status as a parent at all.

English law, as usual, lies somewhere in the middle. Surrogacy arrangements are not illegal in themselves: but commercial intermediaries and advertisements are banned.[45] The surrogate mother, whether partial or full, is always the child's legal mother;[46]

---

[44] Surrogacy Arrangements Act 1985, s. 1(2),(3).
[45] Surrogacy Arrangements Act 1985, ss. 2–4.
[46] Human Fertilisation and Embryology Act 1990, s. 27.

41

usually (although not invariably) her husband (and sometimes even her unmarried partner) will be the child's legal father.[47] The arrangement is always unenforceable;[48] she cannot be made to hand over the child if she changes her mind. But is she does hand him over; there is now a special procedure for putting the surrogacy arrangement into effect.

Previously, the child could only become a member of the commissioning couple's family by adoption; this contravened the bans on direct placement and paying money in return for children, although the courts could waive these retrospectively. Now a court may make a "parental order", transferring the child into their family.[49] As with adoption, only married couples can apply and the child must already be living with them. Unlike adoption, the surrogate parent or parents must agree, unless they cannot be found or are incapable of doing so; there is no provision for dispensing with their agreement on other grounds. No money or other benefit apart from reasonable expenses must have been paid either way, unless the court authorises it. Generally, a guardian *ad litem* will be appointed to advise the court on behalf of the child.

This procedure only applies where the gametes have come from at least one of the commissioning parents. It cannot be used in the other sort of surrogacy, where a woman simply agrees to have a child and hand him over to another couple. It could be used after a do-it-yourself partial surrogacy arrangement, where the commissioning father supplies the sperm either naturally or artificially, although proving all the requirements might be a little difficult.

But full surrogacy would inevitably be covered by the Human Fertilisation and Embryology Act and Code; and these days it is perhaps likely that even for partial surrogacy parents will prefer the safety of a licensed clinic. The Code insists, as does the British Medical Association,[50] that using assisted conception techniques to initiate a surrogate pregnancy should only be considered where it is "physically impossible or highly undesirable for medical

---

[47] *ibid.*, s. 28(2) or (3); see p. 38, above.
[48] Surrogacy Arrangements Act 1985, s. 1A.
[49] Human Fertilisation and Embryology Act 1990, s. 30; Parental Orders (Human Fertilisation and Embryology) Regulations 1994; Family Proceedings Rules 1991, Part IVA.
[50] *Changing Conceptions of Motherhood, The Practice of Surrogacy in Britain*, (1996) British Medical Association.

reasons for the commissioning mother to carry the child."[51] As with sex selection, there is much more sympathy for people who want to interfere with nature for medical reasons than with people who want to do so for social reasons.

The HFEA requires centres to consider the usual welfare of the child criteria in relation to both the surrogate and the commissioning parents, as well as the risks of disruption to the child's early life in the event of any dispute, and the effect upon the existing children in each family.[52] Even if the centre has done all this, it would still be open to the court to refuse to sanction the transfer.

CONCLUSION

The law can, of course, try to ensure that only the right people are allowed to bring up children, not by preventing the children being born, but by removing them from their parents at or after birth. A large part of the work of the Family Division of the High Court, and in county courts and family proceedings courts, consists of these most difficult and anxious cases. It goes without saying that the welfare of the child is the paramount consideration.[53] But it is easy for well-meaning people to think that they are acting in the best interests of the child.[54] In theory the law is opposed to "social engineering". The Children Act 1989 tries to set a threshold of risk before any child can be taken away from home.[55] But this is easier said than done.

Some cases may seem relatively straightforward once the facts have been found. Children need to be rescued from chronic physical or sexual abuse. Others would be straightforward if only we were better at forecasting risk. Should the man who once shot dead his wife and child in cold blood for no apparent reason be denied the chance of ever bringing up a child again? Others involve value judgments which are much more difficult. At what point will the child suffer unacceptable harm through living with parents who are drug addicts, prostitutes, habitual criminals, or

---

[51] Code, para. 3.20.

[52] *ibid.*, para. 3.19.b.

[53] Children Act 1989, s. 1(1).

[54] Those who exported large numbers of children to the Empire and Commonwealth until surprisingly recently must have done so, but see P. Bean and J. Melville, *Lost Children of the Empire* (1989, Unwin Hyman) for a different view.

[55] See s. 31(2).

sometimes all three? And others still involve deciding whether a parent who is mentally ill or physically or mentally disabled can give the child "good enough" parenting.

If it is difficult to decide who should be allowed to keep the children they already have, it would be even more difficult to decide who should be allowed to have them at all. Two propositions seem to make sense. First, if people are able to have children in·the normal way, prior regulation of their right to do so is neither practicable nor justifiable. But they can still be held responsible for the children they have brought into the world; they should not be allowed to pick and choose. Secondly, however, if people want or need help to have children, some prior regulation is both practicable and justifiable.

Perhaps the main justification for both these propositions is not the interests of the individual children themselves. Rather it is the interest which we all have in supporting the essential randomness of nature. This leads us to accept that even the "Sarahs" may have children who will enrich the human race; but that to allow even the most suitable parent to design her own child will impoverish us all in the long run.

3. Matchings

This time it seems that I myself am the bogeywoman. My colleagues and I have featured as the enemies of marriage in articles by such diverse but serious authors as Melanie Phillips[1] and John Patten[2] and perhaps less seriously by William Oddie, John Torode,[3] and Ralph Harris.[4] All were attacking the Family Law Bill 1995–1996 which is based upon two reports published by the Law Commission while I was leading its work in Family Law.[5]

It is flattering to be thought to have had so much influence on the work of a collective. This work was thoroughly researched and consulted upon before it left the Commission. Afterwards, the Report on Domestic Violence and Occupation of the Family Home was scrutinised both by the House of Commons Home Affairs Committee[6] and by the House of Lords through the new "Jellicoe" committee procedure.[7] On the Ground for Divorce, the Government went through essentially the same consultation processes as the Law Commission had done.[8]

It is even more flattering to be accused of having a clear agenda to "call in question the very concepts of marriage and the family", when I am simply trying to puzzle out where some recent social and legal developments may be taking us. It all goes back to a paper I contributed in 1979 to the Third World Conference of the

[1] "Unhappy families on the marry-go-round", *The Observer*, October 29, 1995.
[2] *Daily Telegraph*, September 19, 1995.
[3] "Legal commissars subverting family values", *Daily Mail*, November 1, 1995.
[4] "Divorced from his own party", *The Times*, March 13, 1996.
[5] Law Com. No. 207, *Domestic Violence and Occupation of the Family Home*, 1993; Law Com. No. 192, *Ground for Divorce*, 1990.
[6] House of Commons Home Affairs Committee, *Domestic Violence*, (1992–93, H.C. 245-I).
[7] House of Lords, Family Homes and Domestic Violence Bill [H.L.], Proceedings of the Special Public Bill Committee, Chairman: Lord Brightman, (1994–95 H.L. Paper 55).
[8] Lord Chancellor's Department, *Looking to the future, Mediation and the ground for divorce, A Consultation Paper*, Cm. 2424, 1993; *Looking to the future, Mediation and the ground for divorce, The Government's Proposals*, Cm. 2799, 1995.

International Society on Family Law on Marriage and Cohabitation in Contemporary Societies.[9] The paper analysed the historical development of the English law of marriage and concluded:

> "Logically, we have already reached a point at which, rather than discussing which remedies should now be extended to the unmarried, we should be considering whether the legal institution of marriage continues to serve any useful purpose."[10]

The point is that modern marriage law does indeed serve some very useful legal purposes, mainly in protecting and supporting the younger or weaker members of the family, but these are rather different from its traditional functions. The State, no less than the people involved, might find them just as valid and important for relationships outside marriage. Hence there is a need to clarify what, if any, the distinctive legal purpose of marriage should be. Put another way, is there any longer any necessary connection between the legal concepts of marriage and the family?

None of this was tremendously novel or contentious. The star of the 1979 conference was Professor Mary Ann Glendon, who had already shown how an "unparalleled upheaval" has taken place in the family law systems of western industrial societies.[11] These have all moved away from regulating the making, conduct and breaking of marriage and towards regulating the economic and child-related consequences of both marital and non-marital unions.

Professor Eric Clive, soon to become a Scottish Law Commissioner, was much more radical.[12] He argued that marriage was an unnecessary legal concept. It could remain a private or religious matter, but need have no effect upon the parties' legal relationship. The legal system could ignore marriage altogether, leaving people free to make their own arrangements.

My own view is that marriage is still the best way for the couple

---

[9] See J.M. Eekelaar and S.N. Katz (eds.), *Marriage and Cohabitation in Contemporary Societies, Areas of Legal, Social and Ethical Change* (1980, Butterworths).

[10] "Ends and Means: The Utility of Marriage as a Legal Institution", Chap. 10 in J.M. Eekelaar and S.N. Katz, *op. cit.*

[11] In *State, Law and Family: Family Law in Transition in the United States and Western Europe* (1977, North-Holland).

[12] "Marriage: An Unnecessary Legal Concept?", Chap. 8 in J.M. Eekelaar and S.N. Katz, *op. cit.*

themselves to regulate their affairs. It offers them both very real advantages, but in particular it provides much the best legal protection for the interests of the weaker party, no longer necessarily the woman, and the children. It also serves a great many other social and psychological purposes which have nothing to do with the law. But for whatever reasons, fewer and fewer people are choosing to enter it, whether or not they have children. So the rest of us have to look at how much of that regulation and protection can and should be provided outside marriage.

So my purpose now is to ask what is the role of the law in regulating of adults' love lives? Should people be allowed to make and break their own legal relationships in this area as in any other? Should they be able to choose between different sorts of relationships, in or out of something called marriage? And how far should they be able to choose their own terms for those relationships? What legitimate public interest have we in constraining that choice in some way?

THE GRANDPARENTS' WORRIES

Thelma Fisher's impression of the debates on the Family Law Bill in the House of Lords "is of a grandparent generation's deep anxiety about marriage breakdown ... The elders of the tribe have been grieving and casting about for explanations."[13] There is certainly a great deal to worry about.

Although there are now enough mates to go round, crude marriage rates have fallen to their lowest since records began.[14] Generally, people are thought to be postponing rather than rejecting marriage. Most people will marry eventually. But there has been a sharp rise in the rates of cohabitation: the percentage of non-married women aged 18 to 49 cohabiting rose from 12 per cent to 23 per cent between 1981 and 1994–95.[15] This is usually a prelude rather than an alternative to marriage: as many as half of all marrying couples have lived together before their marriage, and it is now the norm to do so before re-marrying.[16]

This reflects a real change in attitudes. In 1994, only 16 per cent

[13] (1996) 6(1) *Family Mediation* 3.
[14] D. Utting, *Family and parenthood, Supporting families, preventing breakdown* (1995, Joseph Rowntree Foundation), p. 15.
[15] *Social Trends 26* (1996), Chart. 2.13.
[16] Utting, *op. cit.*, p. 15; K.E. Kiernan and V. Estaugh, *Cohabitation, Extra-marital childbearing and social policy* (1994, Family Policy Studies Centre), p. 5.

Matchings

Marriages and divorces

2.17

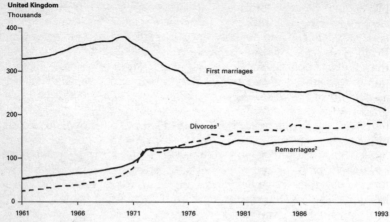

United Kingdom
Thousands

First marriages

Divorces[1]

Remarriages[2]

1961   1966   1971   1976   1981   1986   1993

1 *Including annulments*
2 *For one or both partners*
Source: Social Trends 26 (1996). Crown copyright 1996 Reproduced by permission of the Controller of HMSO and the
Office for National Statistics

Percentage of women[1] cohabiting   2.13

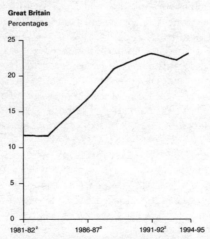

Great Britain
Percentages

1981-82[2]   1986-87[2]   1991-92[2]   1994-95

1 *Non-married women aged between 18 and 49*
2 *Calendar years up to 1988*
Source: Social Trends 26 (1996). Crown copyright 1996
Reproduced by permission of the Controller of HMSO
and the Office for National Statistics

of women and 17 per cent of men thought that living together outside marriage was always wrong; but once again there was a big difference between the generations; only six and seven per cent in the 16 to 34 age group thought this, compared with 40 per cent of those aged 65 or more.[17] The great majority of people in Britain would still advise a young man or woman to marry rather than to live together without marrying, but more than half of these (and many more than half in the younger age groups) would advise living together before marriage.[18] This must worry the elders, not least because the marriages of couples who have lived together beforehand have been more rather than less likely to end in divorce.[19]

There is a growing phenomenon of permanent cohabitation, even after the couple have children. Informal marriage is not new: historians have shown how a sizeable proportion of the population lived together in marriage-like relationships outside the blessing of the ordinary law at least until the middle of the last century.[20] But it has been relatively unusual in this century. This means that it is difficult to make reliable comparisons between people in long-term married and unmarried relationships, as opposed to between married and single people.

There is a good deal of evidence that married people are both physically and mentally healthier than unmarried.[21] For example, premature death is much more common amongst single, widowed and divorced men that it is amongst the married. Of course, there is the usual chicken and egg argument: is it because healthier people get married or because marriage is not only less stressful but also a protection against certain types of health-riskier behaviour?

There is also the his and hers argument. The premature death correlation is nowhere near as strong for women, although it is still there. More than 20 years ago, Professor Jessie Bernard pointed to all the evidence which showed that "there are two marriages,

[17] See *Social Trends 26*, Table 2.15, from the British Household Panel Survey.
[18] J. Scott, M. Braun and D. Alwin, "The family way", in R. Jowell *et al*, *International Social Attitudes, the 10th BSA report* (1993, SCPR).
[19] J. Haskey, "Pre-marital cohabitation and the probability of subsequent divorce" (1992) 69 *Population Trends* 10.
[20] J.R. Gillis, *For Better, For Worse: British Marriages, 1600 to the Present* (1985, Oxford University Press); S. Parker, *Informal Marriage, Cohabitation and the Law 1750–1989* (1990, Macmillan); R.B. Outhwaite, *Marriage and Society: Studies in the Social History of Marriage* (1980, Europa).
[21] F. McAllister, *Marital Breakdown and the Health of the Nation* (1995, One plus One).

then, in every marital union, his and hers. And his … is better than hers."[22] She argued that:

> "At the present time, at least, if not in the future, there is no better guarantor of long life, health and happiness for men than a wife well socialized to perform the 'duties of a wife', willing to devote her life to taking care of him, providing even enforcing, the regularity and security of a well-ordered home."[23]

She went on to argue that the pluses of marriage for men would even be increased by recent developments—wives sharing increasingly in the provider role and a greater tolerance for extra-marital relations. It seems, however, that on this side of the Atlantic at least, she has been wrong about that.

If marriage is on the whole a healthier and happier condition for both men and women, we do not yet know whether the same applies to long-term marriage-like cohabitation. Similar problems of comparison arise when looking at the pluses and minuses for the children. We know a good deal about the differences between living with one and living with two parents, but we know much less about the differences between living with two married and two unmarried parents.[24]

On almost every measure, whether of physical, emotional or educational well-being, children living with two parents are likely to do better than children living with only one.[25] This does not mean, of course, that they are bound to so do. One of the grosser injustices which can be done to children living with only one parent is to take it for granted that they will be damaged by that fact alone. This is almost as bad as blaming them for it, although far too many children are inclined to blame themselves. But that some of them will be damaged, either in the short or the longer term, cannot be doubted.

[22] J. Bernard, *The Future of Marriage* (1976, Penguin Books), p. 29.
[23] *ibid.*, p. 40.
[24] See the comparative study of married and cohabiting mothers by S. McRae, *Cohabiting Mothers* (1993, Policy Studies Institute); also K.E. Kiernan and V. Estaugh, *op. cit.*
[25] For a transatlantic overview of the psychological research, see P.R. Amato and B. Keith, "Parental Divorce and the Well-Being of Children: A Meta-Analysis" (1991) 110 *Psychological Bulletin* 26; for an Anglo-centric overview of the sociological evidence, see L. Burghes, *Lone Parenthood and Family Disruption—The outcomes for the children* (1994, Family Policy Studies Centre).

If a recent Mori survey[26] is to be believed, children themselves believe that "it is better for children to live with both parents rather than one".[27] More than a third of those who lived with both parents worried about their splitting up. Other studies have shown that many children whose parents have separated wish that they were back together again.[28] Even so, most children disagreed with the statement that "children's parents should stay together even if they are unhappy", nor did most of them think that divorce should be made more difficult. Not surprisingly, there were differences between those whose parents were together and those whose parents were apart. There were also differences between boys and girls, with boys being more "conservative" than girls. But more than 80 per cent of them expected to marry.

The children are right to worry about their parents splitting up. The divorce rate[29] in England and Wales increased dramatically immediately after the Divorce Reform Act 1969 came into force. After that, it settled down at a rate which was still higher than previously. But this was not a great deal higher than would be expected under the trend which had already been established before the Act, coupled with those divorces which would have been completely impossible under the old law.[30] Since then it has remained reasonably stable. Even so, the rate per thousand population in the United Kingdom as a whole rose slightly during the 1980s and is now the highest in the European Community.[31] More divorces are now taking place earlier in the marriage. Perhaps because of this, the numbers of children under 16 who are affected by their parents' divorce have risen.[32]

All of this is worrying enough; and the trend towards permanent cohabitation is even more worrying, because there is evidence to support the common sense speculation that cohabiting couples

---

[26] D. Moller, "Do Families Matter?", *Reader's Digest*, November 1995, p. 45, reporting on a survey of 508 children aged 10 to 17.
[27] 77 per cent of those with parents together; 59 per cent of those with parents apart.
[28] *e.g.* A. Mitchell, *Children in the Middle* (1985, Tavistock).
[29] *i.e.* the number of divorces per thousand married people, not the simple numbers.
[30] R. Leete, "Changing Patterns of Family Formation and Dissolution in England and Wales 1964–1976", OPCS Studies on Medical and Population Subjects No. 39, (1979, HMSO).
[31] *Social Trends 26* (1996), Table 2.16.
[32] *Social Trends 26* (1996), p. 59; the matter is complicated, for example, because remarriages have increased but are more likely to fail than first marriages.

2.16

Marriage and divorce rates: EC comparison, 1981 and 1993

Rates per 1,000 population

	Marriages		Divorces	
	1981	1993	1981	1993
United Kingdom	7.1	5.9	2.8	3.1
Denmark	5.0	6.1	2.8	2.5
Finland	6.3	4.9	2.0	2.5
Sweden	4.5	3.9	2.4	2.5
Belgium	6.5	5.4	1.6	2.1
Austria	6.3	5.6	1.8	2.0
Netherlands	6.0	5.8	2.0	2.0
France	5.8	4.4	1.6	1.9
Germany	6.2	5.5	2.0	1.9
Luxembourg	5.5	6.0	1.4	1.9
Portugal	7.8	6.9	0.7	1.2
Greece	6.9	6.0	0.7	0.7
Spain	5.4	5.0	0.3	0.7
Italy	5.6	5.1	0.2	0.4
Irish Republic	6.0	4.4		
EC average	6.1	5.3	1.5	1.7

Source: Eurostat Social Trends 26 (1996). Crown copyright 1996 Reproduced by permission of the Controller of HMSO and the Office for National Statistics

B.2

Women leaving cohabitation: by new marital status, wave one to two and wave two to three

Great Britain   Percentages

	Women cohabiting
Marry partner	16
Partnership dissolves	6
Never married	
Widowed, divorced or separated	3
All leaving cohabitation	25

Source: Social Trends 26 (1996). Crown copyright 1996 Reproduced by permission of the Controller of HMSO and the Office for National Statistics

are far more likely than married couples to split up.[33] Cohabitation is a fragile relationship which ends either in dissolution or in marriage.[34] We do not yet know enough about why couples live together without marrying, still less about what this has to do with the reasons why they split up.

Nor do we know what part, if any, the law plays in all this. The extent to which divorce rates are influenced by the divorce law is controversial enough. To what extent does the legal framework influence people in their choice between marriage and cohabitation? It is unlikely to be simple. The growth in

[33] N. Buck and J. Scott, "Household and Family Change" in N. Buck, J. Gershuny, D. Rose and J. Scott, *Changing Households: The British Household Panel Survey 1990–1992* (1994, ESRC Research Centre on Micro-Social Change).

[34] J. Gershuny *et al*, "British Household Panel Survey", in *Social Trends 26* (1996), Table B.2 shows that a quarter of all cohabitations ended each year, 16 per cent by marriage and 9 per cent by dissolution.

cohabitation outside marriage has coincided with legal changes which ought to have made marriage much more attractive to women. By definition, therefore, they will have made marriage less attractive to men. At the same time, however, marriage has become less socially and economically essential to women. It is scarcely surprising if these powerful forces have combined to loosen its grip on both sexes.

CHOOSING TO MARRY

Historically the law combined with many other pressures to promote marriage as the only legitimate framework for sexual relationships. There were spiritual and sometimes temporal sanctions against any others. People did, of course, live together outside marriage. But for the ordinary law of the land, such relationships were simply irrelevant. Its rules dealt mainly with the acquisition and transmission of property and status. Family relationships for this purpose were created by kindred (blood) or affinity (marriage); but blood only counted if traced through marriage. Even so the law has usually tried to bring as many relationships as possible within the definition of marriage. In medieval times this may have been to save the couple from the sin of fornication.[35] In industrial times the aim is more likely to have been to place responsibility for maintenance upon the individuals rather than the State.[36]

Once a relationship was defined as marriage, the law laid down the terms. The parties did not have a free choice about how they should order their lives. This did not necessarily mean that they knew where they stood. The legal obligations of marriage have never been spelled out in a single statute and are by no means easy to work out. Matters have been complicated because even the private law stemmed from several different sources: common law and equity dealt with the relationship of husband and wife for the purposes of the laws of property, contract, tort and crime; ecclesiastical law dealt with disputes about their marital relationship and became the secular law of divorce and other matrimonial causes; and domestic remedies were eventually introduced in magistrates' courts to cater for the matrimonial problems of the poor. On top of this were the effects of the public

[35] J. Jackson, *The Formation and Annulment of Marriage* (2nd ed., 1969, Butterworths).
[36] S. Parker, *op. cit.*

law, occasionally the criminal law but more often the poor law and its descendants. Law-makers also have a habit of changing the content of the marital bargain with retrospective effect. Reforms have always applied to existing marriages as well as those to come.

"Look it up — nobody knows what it means"

© Pugh/The Times, 1995

The contents of the marital package have altered over the years, depending upon the main legal purpose. Its traditional function was to create and perpetuate kinship networks for the transmission of property, status and power. If this were still its main purpose, nobody would be particularly worried about the present high rate of divorce and growing rate of cohabitation outside marriage. Such people have always gone to lawyers and can arrange their affairs as seems best to them. Marriage is a convenient way of defining who is to benefit from an estate, but there are others.

But this dynastic view of marriage became inconsistent with the economic, social and psychological realities of most families' lives.[37] Economically, these included the shift from the "old" to the "new" property, from land and other corporeal assets to work

---

[37] W.A. Goode, *World Revolution and Family Patterns* (1963, New York, Free Press); *World Changes in Divorce Patterns* (1993, Yale University Press).

and work-related benefits including pensions;[38] this and other factors brought with them the emancipation of the younger generation from their elders' control. Socially, they included the changing role of women at work and at home, their greater participation in the workforce and control over their own fertility. Psychologically they included the values of romantic love for the adults and a happy childhood for the children. In these circumstances, it is not surprising that the legal focus shifted from the long term interests of the dynasty to the security and well-being of the couple and their children.

On the other hand, English law also subscribed to the Christian concept of an exclusive life-long union. The Christian values of protecting the weaker parties looked much better served by a permanent commitment, involving financial and emotional support and a shared obligation to their children, than by the more fragile relationship which would serve for dynastic purposes. But the law was only able to devise and sustain the concept of a life-long union at the cost of gross inequality between the spouses. If the law contributed in any way towards the stability of individual marriages, it did so by putting pressures upon a dependent wife to stay at home which were much greater than those which were put upon the self-sufficient husband to do so.

For some people this must have seemed like the worse of both worlds. Husbands may have found the life-long union irksome because they could not rid themselves of a barren or faithless wife. Wives found it worse than irksome when the sacrifices it undoubtedly brought in their legal status were not compensated by the physical and financial protection it was supposed to bring. Bit by bit, therefore, and always for very good reasons at the time, the ingredients of the old marital bargain have disappeared.

This has not robbed the relationship of all meaning, but it has certainly changed its fundamental character. Generally, now, the focus is on allowing the couple to make what arrangements they please during the marriage; but on overseeing the arrangements they make when it comes to an end; and trying to ensure that these are as fair and suitable as possible both for the parties and for their children.

---

[38] C. Reich, "The New Property" (1964) 72 *Yale Law Journal* 733; its relevance for family law is explored by Mary Ann Glendon in "The New Marriage and the New Property", in Eekelaar and Katz, *op. cit.*, and also in *The New Family and the New Property* (1980, Butterworths, Toronto).

THE EVOLUTION OF EQUALITY

We can trace three broad phases in the development of the law.[39] Before the transfer of the ecclesiastical jurisdiction to the new Court for Matrimonial Causes in 1857 and the Married Women's Property Act of 1882, there was the period of the legally indissoluble union in which the wife's legal personality was almost entirely subsumed in her husband's.

There was then a series of 19th and early 20th century reforms which granted the wife a separate legal personality from her husband and gave them both more effective remedies to enable them to separate or even to divorce and remarry. The conventional view became that these made the husband and wife co-equal partners. As Professor Carol Smart has observed, only by contrasting the law before 1971 with the even worse state of the common law could this possibly have been said.[40] The law did not even give them complete formal equality and their position in fact was usually far from equal.

The present law is mostly the product of a revolution which took place in 1971, when the Divorce Reform Act 1969, the Law Reform (Miscellaneous Provisions) Act 1970 and the Matrimonial Proceedings and Property Act 1970 all came into force. All of these followed the precedent set for the first time by the Matrimonial Homes Act 1967 in making no formal distinction between husband and wife in the remedies available.

If we look in turn at the development of the couple's personal, financial and parenting responsibilities, we can see how the law operated very differently against husband and wife until about 25 years ago. Nowadays, however, it would seem to comply with the requirements of Article 5 of the Seventh Protocol to the European Convention on Human Rights:[41]

"Spouses shall enjoy equality of rights and responsibilities of a private law character between them, and in their relations with their children,

---

[39] There are several historical or sociological treatments of marriage and divorce, including O.R. McGregor, *Divorce in England* (1957, Heinemann); C. Smart, *The Ties that Bind: Law, Marriage and the Reproduction of Patriarchal Relations* (1984, Routledge and Kegan Paul); R. Phillips, *Putting Asunder: A History of Divorce in Western Society* (1988, Cambridge University Press); L. Stone, *Road to Divorce 1530–1987* (1990, Oxford University Press); C. Gibson, *Dissolving Wedlock* (1994, Routledge).
[40] C. Smart, *op. cit.*, p. 29.
[41] Agreed in 1984, but not yet ratified by the United Kingdom.

as to marriage, during marriage and in the event of its dissolution. This shall not prevent States from taking such measures as are necessary in the interests of the children."

Personal responsibilities

Perhaps the most fundamental part of the marital bargain is the promise to live together. The law recognised a long time ago that it could not enforce the duty of matrimonial intercourse, but it did try to enforce their duty to live together.[42] The decree of restitution of conjugal rights ordered a deserting spouse to return. The original penalty for disobedience was excommunication, but in 1813 this was replaced by a power to imprison for contempt.[43] This in turn was abolished in 1884, interestingly in order retrospectively to avoid a husband being imprisoned for failing to return to his wife.[44] After that, it became a peg upon which other matrimonial remedies could depend. The decree itself was abolished in the 1971 reforms; ironically, shortly before that, a wife who had taken the decree at face value and tried to move in with her husband had been forbidden to do so.[45]

The common law had also given the husband various rights to claim damages against third parties who enticed away, harboured, committed adultery with, or otherwise interfered with his right to enjoy his wife's company. Only one of these was ever extended to the wife. They were mostly abolished in 1971, although his right to damages for a tort against her which interfered with his enjoyment of her services and society survived until 1982.

For a time, the common law allowed a husband to use self help to enforce the wife's obligations to live with him,[46] to behave properly, and to have sexual intercourse with him. His right to lock her up was finally laid to rest in 1891,[47] along with his right to

[42] *Forster v. Forster* (1790) 1 *Hag Con* 144, at p. 154; 161 E.R. 504, at p. 508.
[43] Ecclesiastical Courts Act 1813; for an example, see *Barlee v. Barlee* (1822) 1 Add. 301, 162 E.R. 105.
[44] Matrimonial Causes Act 1884, popularly known as "Mrs Weldon's Act" because it was a response to Mrs Weldon's attempt to have her husband committed for contempt; see *Weldon v. Weldon* (1885) 9 P.D. 52. As M. Doggett observes, in *Marriage, Wife-Beating and the Law in Victorian England* (1992, Weidenfeld and Nicolson), p. 105, "It seems that it would have been more accurately dubbed '*Mr* Weldon's Act'!"
[45] *Nanda v. Nanda* [1968] P. 351.
[46] *Re Cochrane* (1840) 8 Dowl. P.C. 630.
[47] *R. v. Jackson* [1891] 1 Q.B. 671, C.A.

chastise her for misbehaviour. The criminal offences of kidnapping and false imprisonment now protect wives as much as anyone else.[48]

So too, in theory, do all the other offences which are designed to protect people from violence. In practice, however, the police and others still subscribed to a policy of non-intervention until well into the 1970s, fearing that to interfere between those bound together in marriage was more dangerous than trying to protect one of them from abuse.[49] The victims themselves also face this same dilemma, which makes these cases particularly frustrating for those who try to help them. But the private law has now developed some more effective remedies[50] and the police policies have changed. Both now recognise that failing to intervene between the weak and the strong amounts to protection of the strong.[51]

The husband's right to oblige her to have intercourse was not abolished until 1991.[52] In upholding the right of the judges to develop the criminal law in this way,[53] the European Court of Human Rights has said:

"... the abandonment of the unacceptable idea of a husband being immune against prosecution for rape of his wife was in conformity not only with a civilised concept of marriage but also, and above all, with the fundamental objective of the Convention, the very essence of which was respect for human dignity and human freedom."

Nowadays, therefore, the law realises that it cannot force the couple either to sleep together or to live together, any more than it will force a person to perform a contract for personal services. However, there are other inducements.

[48] *R. v. Reid* [1973] Q.B. 299.
[49] House of Commons Select Committee on Violence within Marriage, Evidence of Association of Chief Police Officers, (1974–75, H.C. 533-II).
[50] Consolidated and improved in Part IV of the Family Law Act 1996, reproducing with minor amendments the Family Homes and Domestic Violence Bill, Session 1994–5, which could not complete all its stages in time because of last-minute amendments put down in response to a campaign in the *Daily Mail*.
[51] This is the objection to the decision of H.H. Judge Fricker, Q.C., to refuse an injunction where the couple were still living together in *F v. F (Protection from Violence: Continuing Cohabitation)* [1989] 2 F.L.R. 451, although the practical problems in enforcing such orders would be considerable.
[52] *R. v. R.* [1992] 1 A.C. 599.
[53] *S W v. United Kingdom; CR v. United Kingdom, The Times*, December 5, 1995.

Financial responsibilities

The most obvious is the power of the purse. As with more direct coercion, this has always operated more powerfully upon the wife than the husband. The common law gave a husband ownership or control over all his wife's property, in particular her earnings. In return, it did recognise that he had an obligation to support her. But it was for him to decide how to do this. He was only under an obligation to give her separate provision if he had formally agreed to do so or it was entirely his fault that they were apart. Even if it was entirely his fault, there was very little she could do either to ensure that she could support herself or to force him to support either her or their children.

The 19th century reforms removed the husband's rights over the wife's property and income. Separate property gives freedom of choice to those with property and income of their own: but it does not produce equality where most couples divide their roles into breadwinner and homemaker. For much of this century, the homemaker was unlikely to have any property right in the matrimonial home; she had only a personal right to live there which ended with the marriage. Once they separated, she could only rely on her inadequate rights of support.

The remedies to enforce those rights were greatly improved once the secular courts took over from the ecclesiastical in 1857; the divorce court could order the husband to make annual and later periodical payments to the wife but it could do nothing about the ownership of their home and its powers to make capital awards were very limited. These powers remained based upon the principle that the property and income in his name belonged to him alone. His duty to support her was the price he had to pay for the freedom he wanted. Although these remedies were never as rigid as the common law, the wife's claims might be reduced or even extinguished if she was in any way to blame whether before or after the separation. The limited powers granted to magistrates' courts were based upon the more rigid principles of the common law until 1981. She had to be 100 per cent innocent before she could expect any help.

In 1971, the divorce courts were given much wider powers to deal with property and capital as well as to order periodical payments on divorce. For the first time, these made no distinction between husband and wife. The leading case of *Wachtel v. Wachtel*[54]

[54] [1973] Fam. 72, C.A.

decided that the assets and income of both parties could be put into a notional pool and then divided between them in accordance with their respective contributions and their needs. Seen in this light, their matrimonial behaviour would only be relevant if there was such a disparity between them that it would be inequitable to disregard it.[55]

However, the 1971 reforms initially preserved the principle of the life-long commitment: the court had to try to put the parties in the position in which they would have been had the marriage not broken down and each had observed their financial responsibilities towards the other.[56] That principle was abandoned in 1984, ostensibly because it was unattainable.[57] At that time, there was general enthusiasm for the "clean break", which was supposed to allow both husband and wife to go their separate and self-sufficient ways.[58] The court now has both the power to achieve this and the duty to consider whether it can be brought about "without undue hardship" to the dependent spouse.[59]

This was the real death of the life-long commitment involved in marriage. There is now no governing principle, only a long list of factors to be taken into account. In practice, only at the very top (because there is enough to go round) and the very bottom (because the State steps in to fill the breech) are both husband and wife likely to retain their pre-divorce standard of living; but the husband is far more likely to do so than the wife and children.[60] Our law now accepts that a previously dependent spouse should expect to suffer some hardship, as long as this is not "undue".

Parenting responsibilities

The other source of pressure was and is the couple's children. The husband originally had almost absolute rights over them, which the law would enforce for him unless his behaviour towards them had been quite atrocious. The 19th century reforms increased the

[55] See now Matrimonial Causes Act 1973, s. 25(2)(g).
[56] Matrimonial Proceedings and Property Act 1970, s. 5(1), later Matrimonial Causes Act 1973, s. 25(1).
[57] Matrimonial and Family Proceedings Act 1984, s. 3, substituting a new version of the 1973 Act, s. 25.
[58] *Minton v. Minton* [1979] A.C. 593.
[59] Matrimonial Causes Act 1973, s. 25A(2).
[60] See the Australian Law Reform Commission, Report No. 39, *Matrimonial Property*, 1987, Chap. 6, for a valuable account of the research evidence.

remedies available to the mother to challenge him, on the basis of what would be best for the children. But her husband remained their guardian at common law and she could usually only rely on her rights of application to the court once they had separated. If the fault was hers, she was also more likely to be deprived of the care of her children or to suffer the indignity of having to look after them while her husband retained the right to make the big decisions about their future.

It was not until 1973 that a married mother acquired an equal status with the father whether or not they went to court.[61] Statute laid down in 1925 that the welfare of the child is the paramount consideration in any dispute about his upbringing, but only in 1977 did the courts decide that the children's welfare could not be balanced against other considerations, such as putting pressure upon one parent to stay with the other.[62] In practice, it can still be extremely difficult to leave with the children and even more difficult to persuade the courts that they should join you if you leave without them.

ENDING THE RELATIONSHIP

In theory, it was also not until 1971 that a couple could agree to be divorced. The ecclesiastical courts would release couples from the obligation to live together, but only on the basis that one of them had committed a "matrimonial offence", not because they had agreed to live apart. The same approach was adopted when judicial divorce was introduced in 1857. The offences themselves were developed, extended and refined but the basic principle remained, with only minor exceptions, until 1971. Divorce or separation was the penalty which the guilty party had to suffer for his or her crime; alternatively, the guilty party's fundamental breach of the marital bargain relieved the innocent party of his or her own obligations under it.

This did mean that a wife who was completely free of blame could resist a divorce for as long as she liked: but this was only a consolation if her husband was able and willing to provide for her properly. She could not stop him leaving and acquiring at least a moral obligation to a new family. Nor was the law quite as coherent

[61] Guardianship Act 1973, s. 1(1).
[62] *Re K (Minors) (Wardship: Care and Control)* [1977] Fam. 179, C.A.; *cf. Re L (Infants)* [1962] 1 W.L.R. 886, [1962] 3 All E.R. 1, C.A.

as it seemed. Ecclesiastical law might refuse to allow a person who was himself guilty of an offence to obtain a decree,[63] but the court had a discretion to grant a divorce despite this.[64] In the 1930s, A.P. Herbert had lampooned the absurdity of refusing a divorce where both spouses wanted one because each had made a new relationship.[65] But the solution adopted in the Matrimonial Causes Act 1937 was not to introduce divorce by consent, but to expand the range of matrimonial offences available.

After that, the law became more and more complicated as the courts tried hard to make sense of who was really to blame for the marital breakdown. Of course, they only had to do so in disputed cases; although collusion was an absolute bar to divorce until 1963, divorce by consent was readily available, provided that one party was prepared to supply the other with the grounds and not to contest them in court.

Since 1971 the sole ground for divorce has been that the marriage has irretrievably broken down. The intellectual case for this had been made in Lord Walker's dissent to the report of the Royal Commission on Marriage and Divorce in 1956.[66] It was accepted and amplified by the Archbishop of Canterbury's group in *Putting Asunder—A Divorce Law for Contemporary Society in 1966*.[67] The only serious debate was about how to prove it. The Archbishop's group proposed an intimate enquiry into the state of each relationship. The Law Commission,[68] however, argued that this was both impracticable and unlikely to persuade the couple to stay together. The logic even then pointed towards a single, neutral method of proof, such as a comparatively short period of separation. Even that would have been less convenient for some than the old-style "hotel adultery" divorce.

In the end, the 1969 Act provided five possible ways of proving that the marriage had broken down. Three of these seemed to mirror the old matrimonial offences of adultery (with an additional requirement that the petitioner found it intolerable to

[63] See *Forster v. Forster* (1970) 1 Hag. Con. 144; 161 E.R. 504.
[64] Matrimonial Causes Act 1857, s. 31.
[65] See, *e.g.* "Pale, M.R. v. Pale, H.J. and Hume (Queen's Proctor showing cause)", Case 66 in *Uncommon Law, Being 66 Misleading Cases* ... (1935, Methuen).
[66] Royal Commission on Marriage and Divorce 1951–5, Chairman: Lord Morton of Henryton, Cmd. 9678, 1956.
[67] Report of a group appointed by the Archbishop of Canterbury, Chairman: Rt. Rev. R.C. Mortimer, Lord Bishop of Exeter (1966, SPCK).
[68] Law Com. No. 6, *Reform of the Grounds for Divorce—The Field of Choice*, 1966.

live with the respondent),[69] cruelty (now defined as behaviour such that it was unreasonable to expect the petitioner to live with the respondent)[70] and desertion (for two years).[71] But is nonsense to suggest that these were in any way designed to reflect who was really to blame for the marital breakdown. The old rules which had at least tried to do this[72] had gone: a habitual philanderer who regularly beat up his wife and left her destitute can now divorce her for one act of adultery. Even before the Act was passed, the law had begun to realise that it might be unreasonable to expect one spouse to live with the other, although the other could not be blamed for his behaviour, perhaps because he was mentally or physically ill, or he had not meant to cause any harm, but was simply extremely selfish or indifferent.[73] After that, the courts' ideas of what people could reasonably be expected to tolerate developed in line with those of the parties. The scope of the misnamed "unreasonable behaviour" became wider and wider.[74]

There were two true no-fault provisions, designed to fill the principal gaps which the Law Commission had identified in the old law. One catered for couples who wanted to divorce by consent without blaming one another, but it made them live apart for two years before doing so.[75] The other catered for people who could not show "fault", or persuade the other to agree, but had lived apart for five years, so long that their marriage must have broken down;[76] but the other has a special defence if the divorce would cause grave financial or other hardship and it would in all the circumstances be wrong to dissolve the marriage.[77]

In practice, the separation facts have never been as popular in England as was expected. Nearly three-quarters of petitioners rely on adultery or behaviour; getting on for one half rely on behaviour.[78] One obvious explanation is that they find the two-

---

[69] Matrimonial Causes Act 1973, s. 1(2)(a).

[70] *ibid.*, s. 1(2)(b).

[71] *ibid.*, s. 1(2)(c).

[72] *i.e.* the bars which prohibited a spouse from insisting on a divorce if he had caused, contributed to, or forgiven the other's fault, or had committed a fault of his own.

[73] *Williams v. Williams* [1964] A.C. 698; *Gollins v. Gollins* [1964] A.C. 644.

[74] It was also comparatively easier and cheaper to prove until a simple admission in the acknowledgement of service became acceptable proof of adultery.

[75] Matrimonial Causes Act 1973, s. 1(2)(d).

[76] *ibid.*, s. 1(2)(e).

[77] *ibid.*, s. 5.

[78] See, *e.g. Social Trends 26* (1996), Chart 2.21, overleaf.

2.21

Divorces granted: by ground, 1993

England, Wales & Northern Ireland
Percentages

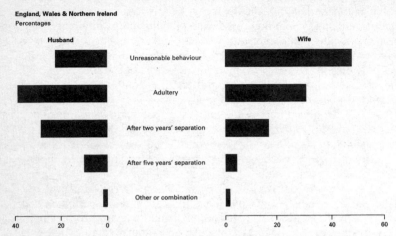

Husband		Wife
	Unreasonable behaviour	
	Adultery	
	After two years' separation	
	After five years' separation	
	Other or combination	

40   20   0   0   20   40   60

Source: Social Trends 26 (1996). Crown copyright 1996 Reproduced by permission of the Controller of HMSO and the Office for National Statistics

year wait too long. Some couples cannot separate before they begin proceedings. Most will not be able to sort out their property and finances until they are divorced. This is because the settlement almost always involves court orders which can only be implemented once they are divorced.

Another explanation is that adultery or behaviour can be and are used to put pressure on the other to agree. It is not too difficult to cobble together a list of allegations which would satisfy the court in an undefended case. Mounting a defence is difficult. The petitioner will then be encouraged to strengthen the allegations. It is hard to think of anything less likely to save a marriage than a fight in open court over the minutiae of their lives together. Spending money on lawyers for this purpose will only diminish what would otherwise be available to support the family. It is rarely thought worth while to spend public money on such a futile exercise.

Another possible explanation for the continued popularity of adultery and behaviour is that there is still a real desire to point the finger of blame at the one seen as the guilty party. The great majority of divorces are undefended but this does not mean that

'We want one of
those old-fashioned
acrimonious divorces'

© The Telegraph plc, London, 1996

both parties are equally anxious to be divorced. The reverse is more often the case. Someone who feels deeply wronged by the other's behaviour may also feel it important to be able to petition for divorce on account of it.

The trouble is that the court has no way of knowing which case is which: is it a tactical move to secure a quick divorce and a possibly more favourable position in the "ancillary" matters, or a genuine and deeply felt reflection of the real reasons why the marriage broke up, or an easy peg on which to hang a consensual divorce? Although the law imposes an obligation upon the court to enquire into the truth of the matter,[79] in practice it cannot do so. A proper enquiry would require either a small army of official investigators and many more judges to consider their reports. The usual reaction to an increase in demand for divorce has been to simplify or downgrade the procedures.[80]

Small wonder that litigants feel a grave sense of injustice at the

---

[79] Matrimonial Causes Act 1973, s. 1(3).
[80] See, *e.g.* S.M. Cretney, " 'Tell me the old, old story'—the Denning Report 50 years on" (1995) 7 *Child and Family Law Quarterly* 163, on the response to the boom in demand which took place after World War II; similarly, the so-called "special procedure" for paper divorce was progressively introduced to cater for demand after the 1969 Act was implemented.

use of these facts.[81] The courts do so, too. Although there certainly are cases in which the parties' behaviour will be relevant in disputes about money or children, this will not be determined by reference to the basis on which the divorce was granted.

It was the dishonesty and injustice of the present law which led to the changes proposed in the Family Law Act 1996, which had such a stormy passage through Parliament in the 1995–6 session. The main aim was to find a more reliable and objective way of proving that a marriage has irretrievably broken down. This could be a period of separation of whatever length is thought to demonstrate that the breakdown is permanent.[82] There is no particular way of knowing how long this might be: it could easily differ from couple to couple. Insisting on separation would make divorce very much harder for some of the more deserving people who currently rely on adultery or behaviour. It also makes it harder for couples to experiment and reconcile. But it is very easy for them to cheat about the date when their separation began. Hence the Law Commission proposed a fixed "cooling off period", during which the couple would be expected to work out the consequences of being divorced before it took place, rather than afterwards as usually happens at present.[83]

It is simply not true that the present law retains the concept of fault in any meaningful way. Nor does it reflect a coherent moral code. It would have been more logical to return to the old law based wholly on the matrimonial offence, but very few people actually want this. Both the Law Commission and the Government found general agreement that irretrievable breakdown of the marriage should remain the basis of the law of divorce; and there was most support for the proposed way of proving this.[84] The second most favoured option was the retention of a "mixed" fault and no-fault system, which is in essence what we have at present. The present law can best be defended on the basis that any change would be worse: it is not at all unknown for the law to mean one thing but say another, for important symbolic purposes.

---

[81] *e.g.*, G. Davis and M. Murch, *Grounds for Divorce* (1988, Oxford University Press).
[82] As has been the law, *e.g.* in Australia since 1975 and was proposed by The Law Society, in *A Better Way Out*, as long ago as 1979.
[83] Law Com. No. 192, *The Ground for Divorce*, 1990.
[84] Law Com. No. 192, paras. 1.7 and 3.5 onwards; Appendix D reports on the results of a public opinion survey. Cm. 2799, paras. 4.1–4.7; Appendix A summarises the results of the Government's consultations.

CHOOSING MARRIAGE TODAY

It is also not true that the Family Law Act will would deprive marriage of all its meaning. The changes which took place in 1971 have made it a much more equal relationship, but it is still one which brings solid benefits to both spouses which others do not.

It allows the couple complete freedom of choice during the marriage to adopt whatever roles or life-styles they see fit. It does not oblige or even assume that one will be the breadwinner and the other the homemaker. They can organise their property and finances as they wish: either by sharing everything or by keeping everything separate or by anything in between.

Its most distinctive feature is that each spouse has an obligation to support the other. Each has an automatic right to live in the matrimonial home irrespective of which of them is the legal owner or tenant.[85] Excluding either of them requires a court order unless he or she agrees to leave. Each spouse can claim reasonable financial provision from the other both during the marriage and if it ends by divorce.[86] If one of them dies without leaving a will, the other automatically succeeds to a substantial "statutory legacy".[87] If that, or the provision made by will, is inadequate, the survivor can apply to the court for reasonable financial provision.[88]

From time to time, the Law Commission have recommended further strengthening of the position of spouses. They have three times proposed that the matrimonial home should automatically be jointly owned unless the couple agree otherwise.[89] More recently, they have proposed that goods and investments bought or money transferred for the couple's joint use and benefit should be jointly owned unless the couple agree otherwise.[90] These proposals have been strenuously resisted. So too was the

---

[85] Matrimonial Homes Act 1983, replacing the Matrimonial Homes Act 1967, to be replaced by Part IV of the Family Law Bill.
[86] Domestic Proceedings and Magistrates' Courts Act 1978, ss. 1, 6 and 7; Matrimonial Causes Act 1973, ss. 22 to 27.
[87] Administration of Estates Act 1925, s. 46(1)(i); the fixed sum is updated from time to time by statutory instrument.
[88] Inheritance (Provision for Family and Dependants) Act 1975, replacing the Inheritance (Family Provision) Act 1938, as amended.
[89] Law Com. No. 52, *First Report on Family Property: A New Approach*, 1973; Law Com. No. 86, *Third Report on Family Property: The Matrimonial Home (Co-ownership and Occupation Rights) and Household Goods*, 1978; Law Com. No. 115, *The Implications of Williams and Glyn's Bank v. Boland*, 1982.
[90] Law Com. No. 175, *Matrimonial Property*, 1988.

Commission's proposal that on intestacy, the surviving spouse should receive the whole estate, subject to the claims of any dependants for reasonable provision for their maintenance.[91]

What is one to make of this reluctance to improve the lot of those spouses, male or female, whose marriages do not break up? This could be seen as a real failure to support the institution of marriage, as can the release from its financial responsibilities, which was allowed by the 1984 Act.[92]

By contrast, the Family Law Act is intended to strengthen rather than to undermine the financial responsibilities undertaken in marriage. The present law allows a couple to be divorced very quickly. They can then spend the next two or three years arguing about their children and their finances. During this time one of them has usually remarried and taken on new responsibilities. Under the Government's modifications to the Law Commission's proposals[93] they will usually have to have decided what is to happen to their children, their property and their finances before they are set free to marry again.

Another major purpose of the Government's proposals is to encourage couples to sort these things out for themselves, rather than to ask the courts to do so for them. In practice, ancillary matters are usually agreed, most often when financial information is exchanged, but through lawyers. The idea of using mediation instead began with disputes over children.[94] There was a sense that everyone suffered if the children's future had to be resolved in court. No-one liked doing it. So attempts were made to help the parents do so themselves. This raised all sorts of issues of principle: in particular, whether the parents should be coerced into negotiating, and whether the mediator should put any pressure upon them to reach a particular kind of agreement. These issues have become even more contentious as mediation has moved from children to "all issues", including the couple's property and finances.

The cardinal principle of mediation is that the parties are in control.[95] they negotiate their own arrangements with the help of

---

[91] Law Com. No. 187, *Distribution on Intestacy,* 1989.
[92] See p. 60, above.
[93] Cm. 2799, paras. 4.26–4.30.
[94] *e.g.* L. Parkinson, *Conciliation in Separation and Divorce* (1986, Croom Helm); T. Fisher (ed.), *Family Conciliation within the UK, Policy and Practice* (2nd ed., 1992, Jordans).
[95] National Family Mediation and Family Mediators' Association, Joint Code of Practice, 1993.

'He's the mediator for Mum and Dad's "no fault" divorce...'

Mac of the Daily Mail

a neutral outsider. This person will not impose a solution upon them, or even guide them towards a particular end, but will help them to communicate with one another, to identify what is agreed and what is not, and to try and agree upon matters in dispute. The idea is that this will lead to settlements with which everyone feels comfortable, which have a better chance of success, and which will cost a great deal less, both financially and emotionally, not only than battles in court but even than arms-length negotiation by lawyers.[96]

But it can be attacked on either side. One side consists mainly of lawyers who believe that there is a right and just result, particularly in money matters, for which each party should fight; they also believe, rightly, that many dependent spouses are at a severe disadvantage, especially against a husband with substantial but complex assets; it is difficult enough to get him to disclose his assets through the courts and would be much harder without their help; and they fear that many will be too frightened of the other spouse to negotiate directly with him. The other side consists of welfare officers or social workers, who believe that the children's interests, let alone their wishes and feelings, can easily be overlooked in agreements reached between the parents.

These are all good reasons why mediation should remain entirely voluntary on both sides, rich or poor, and why mediators should be properly trained to recognise and reject unsuitable cases and to redress any imbalances in others. In the general enthusiasm for alternative dispute resolution of all kinds, we must not lose sight of the fact that some disputes can only be properly resolved by a court; and it may be that there are more of these in the family context than it is convenient to admit.[97]

It is one thing to insist that the courts should be there to do their job, which is to resolve disputes about legal rights, powers and duties which cannot be resolved by the parties themselves. It is quite another thing to thrust the court processes upon the parties whether or not they want or need it. In many divorce cases, there is no real dispute; but the parties have to negotiate their way

---

[96] Major research studies were conducted by the University of Newcastle Conciliation Project Unit, *Report to the Lord Chancellor on the Cost Effectiveness of Conciliation in England and Wales* (1989), and J. Walker, P. McCarthy and N. Timms, *Mediation: The Making and Remaking of Co-operative Relationships* (1994, Relate Centre for Family Studies, University of Newcastle); other relevant studies are discussed in G. Davis, *Partisans and Mediators* (1988, Oxford University Press).
[97] See G. Davis, *op. cit.*

through the complex process of disentangling lives which have been bound together closely for some time.

How much choice should the couple be allowed in the arrangements they eventually make? The financial responsibilities of marriage are there to protect the whole community as well as the parties. "Public policy" has always said that the parties cannot make any agreement which ousts the jurisdiction of the court.[98] The commitment involved in marriage means that in theory the court should oversee the arrangements they have made; hence there is a duty to make full and frank disclosure both the court and to the other party.[99] In principle, this is a far more practicable task than trying to keep the couple together.

In practice, the courts have proved little better at doing this than they have at protecting the status of marriage from those who want to be divorced. They are not equipped to make their own inquiries and so must rely upon what the parties tell them. Orders may be made by consent on the basis of very limited "prescribed information".[1] Where there are no fixed rules, there are no absolutely right solutions. The court is most unlikely to want to interfere with what the parties have agreed between themselves.[2] There is common sense, as well as logic, in taking the job of protecting the public purse away from private litigation between the parties and giving it to a public agency instead; and this is exactly what the Child Support Act 1991 tries to do.

The same problem applies to arrangements for the children. In theory there is a public interest in ensuring that these are, if not in the children's very best interests, at least "satisfactory" or the "best that can be devised in the circumstances". The courts used to be required to evaluate the couple's arrangements in this way.[3] In practice there was little information to go on and little to be done to influence what was agreed.[4] Parents can be expected to think again, and to think very carefully about what will be best, but they

---

[98] *Hyman v. Hyman* [1929] A.C. 601; Matrimonial Causes Act 1973, s. 34(1)(a).

[99] *Livesey (Formerly Jenkins) v. Jenkins* [1985] A.C. 424.

[1] Matrimonial Causes Act 1973, s. 33A, inserted in 1984 in response to *Livesey (Formerly Jenkins) v. Jenkins* [1985] A.C. 424, and Family Proceedings Rules 1991, r. 2.61.

[2] *Dean v. Dean* [1978] Fam. 161.

[3] Matrimonial Causes Act 1973, s. 41; first enacted in the Matrimonial Proceedings (Children) Act 1958, s. 2, in response to recommendations in the Report of the Royal Commission on Marriage and Divorce 1951–6, Cmd. 9678.

[4] Law Commission Working Paper No. 96, *Review of Child Law: Custody*, paras. 4.4–4.16, discuss the research evidence and arguments.

cannot be forced to look after their children in a different way if they do not want to do so. The court can only interfere with what the parties decide for themselves if the children will otherwise be put at risk. Hence the court's role is now to obtain the basic information and decide what, if anything, needs to be done about it.[5] The policy is to encourage the parents to continue to share as much responsibility for their children as possible and only to make orders if these will actually improve matters.[6]

In this way, modern marriage law provides couples with a flexible but committed relationship in which each must accept some responsibility for the other as well as for their children; the new divorce law is designed to reinforce that commitment by making them pause for thought before ending their relationship[7] and by insisting that they make proper arrangements for discharging their mutual responsibilities before they are free to marry again. But it does not try to impose any particular way of life upon them.

CHOOSING TO COHABIT

It is odd that cohabitation outside marriage, and in particular the deliberate rejection of marriage as an institution, should have taken off just when marriage had become so much more flexible and equal. One possible explanation is that, while the balance of advantage between marriage and cohabitation has probably shifted towards marriage for women, it has probably shifted the other way for men.

There is formidable support for this theory. Family law has scarcely been touched at all in the previous 46 years of Hamlyn lectures: the notable exception was Professor Tony Honore's series in 1982, *The Quest for Security: Employees, Tenants, Wives*. He discussed the improved protection given by modern family law to the weaker party on divorce; and he predicted that men would be less willing to marry and that non-marital cohabitation would increase as a result. Controversially, he concluded that "In our pursuit of security for the weak we have overlooked the

---

[5] Matrimonial Causes Act 1973, s. 41, substituted by Children Act 1989, s. 108(4), Sched. 12, para. 31.
[6] Children Act 1989, s. 1(5).
[7] As amended in the Commons, as long as 18 months in most cases.

paradoxical fact that the interests of the weakest often depend upon the security of the strong."[8]

Professor Honore was certainly more accurate than Professor Bernard in predicting developments on this side of the Atlantic; but he accepted that it would be difficult to set up a study to test whether his hypothesis as to the cause of any increase in cohabitation was correct; in any event, he did not expect the impact to be great.

It is unlikely that most people calculate as clearly as this when making or breaking their intimate relationships. Some may reject marriage because they know only too well what it entails and do not want it. Couples where one or both have previously been divorced may well be deterred from marrying by the fear of what they will have to go through in order to be divorced.[9]

Others may have rejected marriage because of what they believe it to be. These beliefs are not necessarily well founded in the law, but the law is not the only or even the main ingredient in the marital relationship: religious, social, cultural and psychological factors may be much more important.[10] Marriage may still be perceived as an unequal institution in which the parties are expected to adopt stereotypical roles from which they will have difficulty escaping: "I don't like the institution of marriage. I find it oppressive. It is a prison once you are married".[11]

The 1989 British Social Attitudes Survey found that cohabiting couples were more likely to voice egalitarian ideas about the division of roles within the relationship than were the married.[12] They were also more likely to report that they shared the domestic tasks equally. Even so, for most couples the woman still does the lion's share of the everyday domestic work.[13] Susan McRae[14] found that "long term cohabiting couples are not noticeably more

---

[8] T. Honore, *The Quest for Security: Employees, Tenants, Wives* (1982, Stevens), p. 117.

[9] S. McRae, *op. cit.*, p. 49.

[10] L. Weitzman, *The Marriage Contract—Spouses, Lovers and the Law* (1981, Free Press).

[11] S. McRae, *op. cit.*, p. 46.

[12] K.E. Kiernan and V. Estaugh, *op. cit.*, p. 20; these comparisons are not reported in K. Kiernan, "Men and Women at Work and at Home" in R. Jowell *et al*, *British Social Attitudes, the 9th report* (1992, SCPR).

[13] The British Social Attitudes Survey has found that the division of tasks became slightly more equal from 1983 to 1991, but remained very unequal, especially for washing and cleaning, and was more unequal than people themselves thought it should be; see *Social Trends 25* (1995), p. 32 and Table 2.7.

[14] S. McRae, *op. cit.*, p. 83.

egalitarian in beliefs than other couples with some experience of cohabitation, nor are they particularly more likely to share household chores." Rather, "it was women who did not live with their husbands outside marriage who stood apart." But both studies found that any differences in practice between married and cohabiting couples shrank to almost nothing once they had children. In all families, having children has a greater impact upon domestic organisation and harmony than does the legal relationship between the adults.

Some may believe that such quasi-marital cohabitation, especially once there are children, brings with it the same legal protection as marriage. The old phrase "common law wife" may have contributed to this. The true position is quite different. Cohabitation brings none of the mutual rights of occupation, support and inheritance between the adults which marriage brings. Cohabiting partners' rights in the family home and other assets depend upon the ordinary principles of property and contract law. These can take some account of the parties' intentions and financial contributions to the acquisition or improvement of the property. But the courts are not allowed to interfere with established rights in order to make reasonable provision for the adults. They can only grant temporary protection and a roof over the family's heads in times of crisis. Their powers to do this will be improved when Part IV of the Family Law Act 1996[15] becomes law, but will still fall far short of what can be done for married couples if they divorce.

The lack of responsibility between the adults contrasts with their shared responsibilities once they have children. The courts' powers to oblige them to provide for their children are now virtually identical to those of married parents.[16] This can include an element to provide for the caring parent, although in practice this is never as much as a spouse could expect.[17] If the children are dependent on public funds, the obligation will be defined and enforced under the Child Support Act 1991; the calculation will take into account the support payable for the parent with care. Public law has long imposed upon both parents an obligation to maintain their children, so as to reduce the burden on public funds.[18]

[15] See p. 76, below.
[16] Children Act 1989, s. 15, Sched. 1.
[17] *Haroutunian v. Jennings* [1980] F.L.R. 62; *A. v. A. (A Minor: Financial Provision)* [1994] 1 F.L.R. 657.
[18] Social Security Administration Act 1992, s. 78(6).

Although the mother alone is automatically legally responsible for the looking after the child, the father can easily share this responsibility with her, either by agreement or by court order.[19] Almost any unmarried father who has shown some commitment to his children, who has established a relationship with them, and who seems to have good reasons for making the application will be granted it.[20] Although an order does not follow automatically if he is granted contact with them,[21] in practice it will usually do so. Even if he is in no real position to meet his responsibilities, perhaps because he is not able to see the children, he may still be given parental responsibility as a mark of his relationship and status.[22] The financial commitment he has made to his children seems to play little part in these decisions.[23] Once granted, parental responsibility is rarely taken away.[24]

It follows that living together without being married is still a comparatively bad deal, especially for the partner who compromises his or her employment or career in order to look after the other partner, their home and their children. By contrast, the father is very little worse off than a married father in relation to his children. Men can now obtain what used to be one of the principal attractions of marriage, a legal relationship with their children, without incurring its obligations to the other parent.

But if the main legal benefits of marriage are the mutual support obligations between the spouses, women now have much less need of this. This is not only because of the improvements in their own economic circumstances, for these have been much less than was hoped in the heady days of the equal pay and sex discrimination legislation on the early 1970s. It is also because of the decline in the economic circumstances of men, particularly in certain socio-economic groups. What, it may be thought, is the point of taking on a husband, if he still has all the traditional

[19] Children Act 1989, ss. 2(2) and 4.
[20] The leading case is *Re H (Minors) (Local Authority: Parental Rights) (No. 3)* [1991] Fam. 151, C.A.; the authorities are fully rehearsed *Re S (Parental Responsibility)* [1995] 2 F.L.R. 648, C.A.
[21] As it does if there is an order that they are to live with him: 1989 Act, s. 12(1).
[22] *e.g. Re H (A Minor) (Parental Responsibility)* [1993] 1 F.L.R. 484, C.A.; it should be looked on as a matter of status rather than rights, *Re S (Parental Responsibility)* [1995] 2 F.L.R. 648, C.A.
[23] *Re H (Parental Responsibility: Maintenance)*, [1996] 1 F.L.R. 867, C.A.
[24] *Re P (Terminating Parental Responsibility)* [1995] 1 F.L.R. 1048.

expectations of his wife but is unable to fulfil her traditional expectations of a husband?[25]

DEVELOPING COHABITATION LAW

It would a bold commentator who felt able to choose between these, and no doubt other, possible explanations for the recent rise in cohabitation outside marriage. But what, if anything, should the law be doing about it?

The approach adopted by the law reformers so far has been to consider on a case-by-case basis whether a particular remedy should be extended to unmarried couples. Sometimes this is relatively straightforward. Effective protection against family violence and abuse ought to be available to couples and their children whatever the marital relationship between the adults. More controversially, it is sometimes necessary to keep a roof over the family's head while longer-term solutions are found. This has been recognised by the law since 1976.[26] Part IV of the Family Law Act 1996 contains various provisions designed to clarify, rationalise and in places improve the remedies which already exist.[27] In particular it spells out when a cohabitant or former cohabitant may apply to stay for a while in the home even though he or she has no existing right to occupy it.[28] But when dealing with these applications, the court will be specifically required to take into account that the couple have not "given each other the commitment involved in marriage".[29] The Bill also contains powers to transfer secure tenancies between spouses and cohabitants,[30] principally because there may be no other way of breaking the deadlock.

But there are real difficulties in extending the longer term remedies which impose obligations upon the adults towards one another. It is easy to see why they should both be made to take

[25] *e.g.*, P. Hewitt, *Re-inventing Families*, The Mishcon Lecture, University College, London, May 10, 1995.
[26] Domestic Violence and Matrimonial Proceedings Act 1976; *Davis v. Johnson* [1979] A.C. 264.
[27] Derived from Law Com. No. 207, as generally improved upon in the Family Homes and Domestic Violence Bill, session 1994–5.
[28] Family Law Act 1996, ss. 36, 38 and 41; *cf.* the remedies given to spouses and former spouses in ss. 33–35, and 37.
[29] *ibid.*, s. 41.
[30] *ibid.*, s. 53 and Sched. 7.

responsibility for the children they have brought into the world. But what moral reasons can there be for saddling them with responsibility for one another? It could well be said that it is only marriage which does this. The marriage ceremonies certainly do not spell this responsibility out either accurately or at all. But even if few understand exactly what marriage entails when they undertake it, they must know that it involves a potentially life-long commitment with at least some financial responsibility towards the other party.

It is ironic, therefore, that just as the Family Homes and Domestic Violence Bill (precursor to Part IV of the Family Law Act) was being attacked for something that it did not do—give cohabitants the same property rights as married people— Parliament was passing the Law Reform (Succession) Act 1995.[31] This makes it possible for a cohabitant of two years' standing to apply to the court for reasonable provision from the estate of a partner who has died. Parliament had previously recognised that a cohabitant may suffer financial loss if a partner is wrongfully killed.[32] But this is the first legislation to accept that cohabitation as such, rather than actual dependency, may give rise to legitimate expectations of continued support from the other party. In practice, of course, without showing some dependence the applicant is unlikely to have much of a claim in any event.

English law has been reluctant to spell out the principles governing the financial responsibilities of married couples towards one another. We have already seen how the principle of pretending that the marriage had not broken down was abandoned in 1984. It is difficult, therefore, to decide how much of the same law could be applied to people who have not made the commitment involved in marriage. Scots matrimonial law, by contrast, does spell out some principles.[33] Some of these might be though to depend upon a prior commitment or undertaking of responsibility—the equal sharing of matrimonial property, the gradual transition from dependence to independence, or the relief from serious financial hardship. One—the fair sharing of the economic burden of child care—might be though applicable to all parents, whether or not they have ever married or cohabited with

---

[31] Adding a new s. 1A to the Inheritance (Provision for Family and Dependants) Act 1975; implementing in this respect the recommendations of Law Com. No. 187, Part IV.
[32] Fatal Accidents Act 1976, s. 1(3)(b).
[33] Family Law (Scotland) Act 1985, s. 9.

one another. But one—that "fair account should be taken of any economic advantage derived by either party from contributions by the other, and of any economic disadvantage suffered by either party in the interests of the other party or of the family"[34]—could, as the Scottish Law Commission found,[35] apply equally to unmarried couples. One person may, for example, have voluntarily abandoned an independent place in the world of employment, pensions and contributory benefits and another may have voluntarily accepted domestic services and even been enriched by them. This principle acknowledges that unmarried couples have responsibilities towards one another which arise from their family life together whatever the content of their initial bargain.

COHABITATION AND MARRIAGE CONTRACTS

One view is that there is no need for the law to take any steps, either to counteract or to adapt to the growth of cohabitation. Young people today welcome the greater equality within marriage and relationships generally,[36] and they may also welcome the greater choice of relationship available. The last thing they may want is to have the consequences of marriage thrust upon them. They should be left to arrange their legal affairs by mutual agreement according to the ordinary principles of the law of contract and of trusts.[37] These days, the courts are unlikely to strike down a cohabitation agreement because it promotes an immoral purpose.

This would be all very well if every couple knew exactly what those choices were and the consequences of making them. But of course they do not. Very few cohabiting couples enter into formal agreements with one another dealing with what is to happen if the relationship breaks down. More and more are likely to own or rent a home together, but the processes of settling any disputes about what is to happen to it if they separate are even more cumbersome than those when couples divorce. There is a particularly severe problem, not only for them but also for the

---

[34] *ibid.*, s. 9(1)(b).
[35] Scot Law Com. No. 135, *Report on Family Law,* 1992, paras. 6.14–6.23.
[36] H. Wilkinson and G. Mulgan, *Freedom's Children: Work, relationships and politics for 18–34 year olds in Britain today* (1995, Demos), p. 80.
[37] R. Deech, "The Case against Legal Recognition of Cohabitation" in J.M. Eekelaar and S.N. Katz, *op. cit.*

landlord, if the couple have a joint secure public sector tenancy;[38] no doubt this is why the Family Law Act 1996 still contains powers for the courts to break the deadlock.[39] But the proposal to extend to these couples the simple procedure devised in 1882 for resolving property disputes between married couples[40] was dropped from the Family Homes and Domestic Violence Bill when it became part of the Family Law Bill. This can only add to their financial problems, particularly if they are caught in a negative equity trap.

Long-term cohabiting couples are also less likely to have formal qualifications and more likely to be poor.[41] They are probably less likely to consult lawyers at the outset although they are perhaps more likely to be able to do so when things go wrong. But this puts public money into the lawyers' pockets rather than theirs.

Even if they do consult lawyers at the outset, how likely is it that the arrangements agreed upon then will seem just as fair to them at the end of their relationship, in the light of everything that has happened while they are together? Children, unemployment, relocation, family commitments, changes in taxation or benefits or the ordinary law, and many other things, may have combined to make matters look entirely different.

Exactly the same problems arise in relation to pre-marriage contracts. We have seen how the law is now quite happy to allow married couples to order their lives as they see fit during the marriage. It will usually endorse whatever agreement they reach to re-order their affairs when it ends. But it will not recognise and enforce at the end of the marriage a bargain that they made at the beginning. Even a traditional marriage settlement can be varied on divorce.[42] Those who argue for greater recognition of such contracts agree that there should be "break clauses" allowing renegotiation in certain events.[43] It is difficult to see how such events could not include the breakdown of the marriage itself. This will bring with it so many consequences which could not have been foreseen at the wedding. As we have also seen, law-

[38] *Ainsbury v. Millington* [1986] 1 All E.R. 73, C.A.
[39] s. 53 and Sched. 7.
[40] Married Women's Property Act 1882, s. 17; see Family Homes and Domestic Violence Bill, session 1994–5, clause 20.
[41] J. Ermisch, *Premarital Cohabitation, Childbearing and the Creation of One Parent Families* (1995, ESRC Research Centre on Micro-social Change, University of Essex); see also Kiernan and Estaugh, *op. cit.*
[42] Matrimonial Causes Act 1973, s. 24(1)(c), (d).
[43] The Law Society, *Maintenance and Capital Provision on Divorce* (1991), paras. 3.23–3.56.

By Merrily Harpur

makers have a tendency to change the prescribed content of the marital bargain, sometimes quite dramatically, with retrospective effect. If they can do so, surely the parties must be given the same opportunity.

GAY RELATIONSHIPS

One way of testing our approach to marital and non-marital heterosexual relationships is to ask ourselves how many of the same principles might apply to gay and lesbian relationships. Such questions are relatively new on the Family Law agenda in this country. Until quite recently[44] sexual intercourse between males was a serious criminal offence in England and Wales. Complaints that such laws violated the right to respect for private life under Article 8 of the European Convention on Human Rights were routinely found inadmissible during the 1950s and 1960s. The climate began to change in the 1970s, culminating with the Court's decision in 1981,[45] that the total prohibition in Northern Ireland was a breach of Article 8(1) which could not be justified under Article 8(2) as "necessary in a democratic society" either for the protection of "morals" or "the rights and freedoms of others".

[44] Sexual Offences (Amendment) Act 1957.
[45] *Dudgeon v. U.K.*: Series A No. 45; (1981) 4 E.H.R.R. 149.

But that does not mean that same-sex couples have to be accorded the same rights and duties as married or unmarried opposite sex couples. Freedom from interference with one's "private life" is one thing; giving it the same respect as is due to one's "family life" under the Convention is another. So far, the Commission has not recognised that the relationship of a same-sex couple, whether or not they have children, constitutes their "family life".[46] In similar vein, the European Court has held that Article 12 protects "the traditional marriage between persons of opposite biological sex".[47]

Attitudes to homosexuality are a noticeable exception to the generally liberal trend of public opinion in recent years. Very few people think that homosexuals should have the right to marry.[48] But English law is beginning to recognise these relationships, not so much in their own right, but as an example of a type of relationship which may warrant the grant of a family law remedy.

There is an obvious case for this where the couple have children. The court can already make an order that a child is to live with two people, who happen to be homosexual partners, and this will give them both parental responsibility for the child for as long as the order is in force; it will not, however, impose a financial liability to maintain the child upon anyone other than a parent.[49] If there is a dispute, the courts do not ignore the possible impact upon the child of living in such a household; it is an "important factor" to be taken into account;[50] but they will listen to the evidence about this;[51] and they do not inevitably assume that an alternative home will be better for the child.

There is also a case for protection against violence and other

---

[46] See, *e.g., Simpson v. U.K.*: (No. 11716/85) (1986) 46 D.R. 274.

[47] *Cossey v. U.K.*: Series A No. 184; (1990) 13 E.H.R.R. 622; also *Rees v. U.K.*: Series A No. 106; (1986) 9 E.H.R.R. 56.

[48] Scott, Braun and Alwin, *op. cit.*, p. 40; interestingly 24 per cent in Eire thought that they should have this right, compared with only 12 per cent in Britain.

[49] *cf. Kerkhoven v. The Netherlands* (No. 15666/89) (May 19, 1992) where the Commission found no interference and no discrimination when a lesbian woman was refused parental authority over her partner's child by donor insemination: "as regards parental authority over a child, a homosexual couple cannot be equated to a man and woman living together".

[50] *C v. C (A Minor) (Custody: Appeal)* [1991] 1 F.L.R. 223, C.A.; but on a retrial with psychiatric evidence the mother succeeded.

[51] *e.g.* S. Golombek, A. Spencer and M. Rutter, "Children in Lesbian and Single Parent Households: Psychosexual and Psychiatric Appraisal" (1983) 24(4) *J. Child Psychology and Psychiatry* 551.

forms of molestation. The Law Commission gave this explanation of the need for family members to have special protection, different from the ordinary law of tort:

> "the proximity of the parties often gives unique opportunities for molestation and abuse to continue; the heightened emotions of all concerned give rise to a particular need for sensitivity and flexibility in the law; there is frequently a possibility that their relationship will carry on for the foreseeable future; and there is in most cases the likelihood that they will share a common budget, making financial remedies inappropriate."[52]

The Family Law Act 1996 therefore gives improved remedies against violence and other forms of molestation to all non-commercial homesharers;[53] gay and lesbian couples are included in this concept, but not within the definition of "cohabitant"; this is limited to "a man and a woman who ... are living together as husband and wife".[54] An owner or tenant homesharer can also ask the courts to decide who is to live in their family home in the short term when the relationship goes badly wrong and one needs protecting from the other.[55] But only cohabitants can ask for that protection even if they are not an owner or tenant of the home or for the transfer of secure tenancies when the relationship breaks up.[56]

A similar distinction is drawn in the Inheritance (Provision for Family and Dependants) Act 1975; a gay or lesbian partner may claim reasonable provision for his maintenance if he or she can show dependence upon the deceased; but they will not fall within the new category of cohabitant who can make such a claim without having to prove dependence.

In this way the law is beginning to recognise that gay and lesbian relationships can have a family character. But the courts have had trouble including them within the term "family" when it appears in legislation without a definition. Perhaps this is not surprising, given that Parliament has banned local authorities from promoting the teaching "of the acceptability of homosexuality as a pretended family relationship". So far, a lesbian partner has not counted as a

[52] Law Com. No. 207, para. 3.19.
[53] 1996 Act, ss. 42 and 62(3)(c).
[54] *ibid.*, s. 62(1)(a).
[55] *ibid.*, s. 33.
[56] *ibid.*, ss. 36, 38 and 53, and Sched. 7.

family member who can succeed to a secure tenancy when her partner dies.[57]

Why should homosexual couples not be able to undertake such a relationship, either through marriage or through some appropriately modified form of permanent legal commitment? As yet, this has scarcely been discussed in this country;[58] but such couples are allowed to marry in the Netherlands and to enter into registered partnerships in the Nordic countries.

At present even a transsexual marriage is not recognised here. The parties must be respectively male and female.[59] For this purpose they retain the sexes they had at birth even if one has since undergone sexual re-assignment.[60] Paradoxically, this means that a person who wishes to formalise a homosexual relationship after a sex-change operation may do so.[61]

This brings us back to the purposes of the legal institution of marriage. The European Court may consider that the main purpose of protecting marriage is to protect the right to found a family. Yet this has never been the sole purpose of marriage in English law: if it had been so, the inability to bear children would have been a disqualification.[62] Since the Reformation, even the inability to have sexual intercourse has not been a disqualification unless the parties themselves complain. The role of marriage in establishing the blood line for the purposes of inheritance has also lost most of its importance. The role of providing for the mutual support and protection of the parties no longer differentiates between the husband and the wife. Technically, removing the requirement that the parties be respectively male and female would create few problems.

Despite everything, marriage itself is still greatly valued. Sometimes it is said that it is weddings, rather than the marital relationship they create, which are so popular.[63] No doubt this is partly because we all enjoy a good party and an excuse for dressing

---

[57] *Harrogate Borough Council v. Simpson* [1986] 2 F.L.R. 91; again, the European Commission found that there was no violation of Art. 8 and no discrimination under Art. 14, *Simpson v. U.K.* (No. 11716/85) (1986), 46 D.R. 274. In practice, local authorities may be advised to take a different view.

[58] But see C. Lind, "Time for lesbian and gay marriages?" (1995) 145 N.L.J. 1553; and M. Bowley, "A too fragile social fabric?" (1995) 145 N.L.J. 1883.

[59] Matrimonial Causes Act 1973, s. 11(d).

[60] *Corbett v. Corbett (orse Ashley)* [1971] P. 83.

[61] S. Whittle, "Transsexuals and Marriage" (1996) 146 N.L.J. 379.

[62] See p. 16, above.

[63] J.R. Gillis, *op. cit.*

up. But it is far more significant than that; couples want a rite of passage, a public mark of their commitment to one another, and a symbol of the uniting of their two family trees.[64] Some people think this so important that they do not get married because they cannot afford the wedding.[65]

These symbolic functions could be just as important for gay couples. There is, however, nothing to stop anyone from devising their own ceremonies for this purpose. In fact, there is reason to believe that some heterosexual couples deliberately go through marriage ceremonies which they regard as binding but which are not recognised in English law so that they can avoid the consequences of marriage in English law. The legal ceremony need only become available to gay couples if the legal consequences of marriage are also wanted or needed. It may be that, rather than wishing to contract into a legal relationship designed with heterosexual couples in mind, many would prefer to devise their own. But this brings us back to the difficulties of insisting that people who end their relationships abide by the terms they agreed at the beginning.

STATE'S INTEREST

The real issue remains how far the law should go in imposing its own ideas of the right way to arrange and re-arrange our intimate relationships. It cannot rely entirely on what the couple themselves choose their relationship to be. It has never done so in marriage and the reasons for this can apply just as much to other relationships.

We now allow married couples a great deal of freedom to arrange their own affairs in the way that they want while they are still together. When things go wrong, we try to prevent them doing too much damage to one another and their children. We also try to enforce their financial responsibilities towards one another and to their children. And both the present and the future divorce laws give them some incentive to pause for thought about their own and their children's future.

There is no real reason why a similar combination of choice and responsibility should not be adopted in other relationships. The

[64] P. Mansfield and J. Collard, *The Beginning of the rest of your Life? a portrait of newly-wed marriage* (1988, Macmillan).
[65] S. McRae, *op. cit.*, p. 47.

grandparents' generation, to which I belong, has to be realistic about what the law can and cannot do. As Wilkinson and Mulgan[66] say of today's 18 to 34 year-olds:

> "It is worth remembering that the majority of this generation is still getting married, still having children, and still (just about) managing to maintain long term relationships."

Moreover, they welcomed the recent changes in the style of personal relationships:

> "In our qualitative research we found that young people value the greater equality, mutual respect and intimacy that recent years have brought ... we found a strong optimistic consensus amongst 18–34 year olds that the world of relationships and families has improved greatly compared to their parents' generation."

Modern young people are not going to stand for laws which return to the inequalities of the past. They are not going to get married unless they want to do so. But they will certainly continue to have relationships outside marriage if they want to do so. A proportion of these will be same-sex relationships. If we concentrate on closing the stable door after the horse has bolted we may lose the chance of creating a legal environment in which family life can continue to flourish and develop into the future.

[66] *Op. cit.*, pp. 79–80.

'The Law Commission has come up with a wonderful solution — now, which one of you would like to volunteer for euthanasia?'

Mac of the Daily Mail

4. Dispatchings

The very title to this talk is shocking: of course the law does not countenance the deliberate taking of another's life. But this is not as simple as it seems. The law respects the right to life, as is required by Article 2 of the European Convention on Human Rights.[1] Yet the law also gives us the right to choose what shall be done with our own bodies. It is hard to think of two more fundamental principles of the common law. But, as the case law shows, they can be difficult to reconcile with one another.

A DUTY TO STAY ALIVE?

There is a fundamental difference between the choices involved at the end of life and those involved at the beginning. On the face of it, the choice of when and how to end one's life involves only oneself. We do not owe a legal duty to anyone else to keep on living indefinitely,[2] whereas we do have some responsibilities towards the children we bring into the world and towards the adults with whom we share our lives. It might be thought, therefore, that individual choice would be given greater respect here than elsewhere. In fact, it is not.

This is scarcely surprising. The choice between life and death is irrevocable. The pressures upon anyone who has to decide, whether for themselves or for anyone else, are enormous. Advances in medical treatment and care have greatly increased the range and complexity of the choices available. They have also contributed to the demographic facts which add to the pressures facing all decision-makers.

Both the numbers and the proportions of elderly and aged people in the population have increased considerably. The percentage of people aged 65 and over rose from just under 12 per cent in 1961 to 16 per cent in 1994 and is predicted to rise to around

[1] See p. 94, below.
[2] There is one possible qualification to this statement: see p. 114, below.

Dispatchings

1.1

Population aged 60
and over: by age

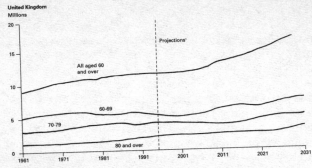

United Kingdom
Millions

Projections[1]

All aged 60
and over

60-69

70-79

80 and over

1961   1971   1981   1991   2001   2011   2021   2031

1 1992-based projections
Source: Social Trends 26 (1996). Crown copyright 1996 Reproduced by permission of the Controller of HMSO and the Office for National Statistics

1.5   ## Dependent population: by age

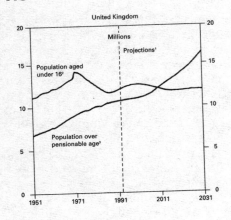

United Kingdom

Millions

Projections[1]

Population aged
under 16[2]

Population over
pensionable age[3]

1951   1971   1991   2011   2031

1 1991-based projections.
2 Data for 1951 to 1971 relate to population under 15
   (the school-leaving age was raised in 1972).
3 Males aged 65 and over, females aged 60 and over.
Source: Social Trends 24 (1994). Crown copyright 1994 Reproduced by permission of the Controller of HMSO and the Office for National Statistics

23 per cent in 2031; but the increase in people aged 80 and over is much sharper, from two per cent, to four per cent, to seven per cent respectively.[3] This has a serious and developing effect upon the dependency ratio, that is the proportion of the population not currently economically active, counterbalancing and at times outweighing the effect of falling birth rates.[4] On the one hand, a good deal has been said about "grey power"; on the other, there is much concern about how their pensions are to be financed and their care provided.[5] This could put at risk the 20th century contract between the generations—that the economically active will support those whose activity is over.[6]

Against this background, the choices made by legislators, courts and health care providers, not themselves in the dependent age groups, require careful scrutiny. So too do the choices made by older people themselves. Not all of us will be as robust as the gentleman shown on page 5. We too may be influenced by questions of cost, of not wanting to be a burden on anyone, or of wanting to be able to have something to pass on to the next generation.

The policy debates on this subject are usually about the relative weight to be given to three principles—individual freedom of choice (autonomy), what others think will be best for the individual (paternalism), or a transcending respect for the value (or sanctity) of human life. If we were to give priority to individual autonomy we would still have to be satisfied that a person has made a real choice. Some people think that the pressures are so great and the decision so momentous that this could never be so. Others may think that there is no difference in kind from the pressures which are faced by people with other very difficult personal decisions to take. We do have to beware dressing up paternalism as respect for the reality of a person's choice. But many people would prefer to give priority to paternalism in any event.

Even if we prefer autonomy to paternalism, it does not follow that this is the only value to be respected. We may respect the

[3] Central Statistical Office, *Social Trends 26* (1996), Chart 1.1, Table 1.5.
[4] Central Statistical Office, *Social Trends 24* (1994) Chart 1.5.
[5] *e.g.* F. McGlone and N. Cronin, *A crisis in care? The future of family and state care for older people in the European Union* (1994, Family Policy Studies Centre).
[6] *e.g.* A. Walker, "Whither the Social Contract? Intergenerational Solidarity in Income and Employment", in D. Hobman (ed.), *Uniting Generations: Studies in Conflict and Co-operation*, (1993, ACE Books).

wishes of someone who genuinely and freely wishes to die. But this does not mean that we recognise only the people who are able to make such choices as valuable human beings. People who cannot choose for themselves need others to protect, not only their best interests, but also their right to respect for their own human individuality. Many would agree with Janet Daley that:

> "To move from the religious idea that what sanctifies human beings is the possession of an immortal soul, to the rationalist one that the only thing that is sacred—the only thing that gives us a right to live—is a fully functioning mind, is a moral shift of considerable significance."[7]

Later on, I shall suggest that we can respect the right to go on living, and acknowledge our responsibility to help other people to do so, without necessarily enforcing a duty to go on living against people who no longer want to go on.

SOME PROBLEMS OF LAW-MAKING

Another difference between this area and the others is that this is still governed almost entirely by the common law. Parliament has intervened very little so far. Some of the judges would like it to do so. The courts in this country have not yet been faced with a request from a physically helpless patient to have his life support systems withdrawn. But a clear indication of what the answer would be was given by the House of Lords in the case of *Airedale NHS Trust v. Bland*.[8] This was about the different but no less difficult question of whether a hospital could stop artificially feeding a young man who had been in a persistent vegetative state (PVS) since being crushed in the crowds at the Hillsborough football ground in 1989. Lord Browne-Wilkinson made a plea for legislative guidance:[9]

> "Where a case raises wholly new moral and social issues, in my judgment it is not for judges to seek to develop new, all-embracing principles of law in a way which reflects the individual judges' moral stance when society as a whole is substantially divided on the relevant moral issues ... For these reasons it seems to me imperative that the

[7] J. Daley, "Where's mercy in such killings?", *Daily Telegraph*, April 16, 1996.
[8] [1993] A.C. 789; see p. 104, below. The Scottish courts have recently reached a similar conclusion but by a different route: *Law Hospital NHS Trust v. Lord Advocate and Another*, *The Times*, May 20, 1996.
[9] *ibid*., at p. 880.

moral, social and legal issues raised by this case should be considered by Parliament."

There are many theoretical arguments in favour of legislation: certainty versus the capacity for organic growth; coherence versus the need to adapt to new circumstances; and above all, democratic legitimacy versus the views of individual judges. In practice, however, the most carefully constructed, thoroughly researched and consulted upon, consensus-seeking proposals can founder for political reasons which have little to do with their intrinsic merit or acceptability to the general public.

Both the English[10] and the Scottish[11] Law Commissions have recently proposed comprehensive legislative schemes for making all kinds of decisions on behalf of people who are unable to make decisions for themselves. These would cover people like Anthony Bland, who had not said anything about what he would like to happen to him before catastrophe struck. They would also cover people such as Jehovah's Witnesses who give a clear indication of what they do, or more often do not, want to happen. They are meant to provide a framework for decision making which reflects the principles established in the present law. But the Government has been understandably cautious in its response.[12] In practice, therefore, the judges are unlikely to get the clear guidance that they seek for some time to come, if at all.

Some are quite comfortable with the traditional case by case approach of the common law. In another recent case about the courts' power to make decisions about someone who was unable to decide for himself, Sir Thomas Bingham M.R. said:[13]

> "This is pre-eminently an area in which the common law should respond to social needs as they are manifested, case by case. Any statutory rule, unless framed in terms so wide as to give the court an almost unlimited discretion, would be bound to impose an element of inflexibility which would in my view be wholly undesirable."

Even so, there are limits to what this approach can achieve. That case was simply a development of the principles governing the care and treatment of incapacitated people, laid down by the

---

[10] Law Com. No. 231, *Mental Incapacity*, 1995.

[11] Scot Law Com. No. 151, *Report on Incapable Adults*, 1995.

[12] Lord Chancellor's Department Press Notice, *Lord Mackay Responds to Law Commission Report on Mental Incapacity*, January 16, 1996; *Hansard* (H.C.), Vol. 269, Written Answers, January 16, 1996, cols. 489–90.

[13] *Re S (Hospital Patient: Court's Jurisdiction)* [1996] Fam. 1, at p. 19G.

House of Lords in *Re F (Mental Patient: Sterilisation)*.[14] Lord Goff, at least, had based these upon a concept of necessity. But it is difficult to imagine that the English judiciary either could or would develop the concept of necessity as the Dutch have done, so as to define the circumstances in which doctors may help their patients to die.[15] In the meantime, they will respond as best they can to the particular cases presented to them within the framework of the existing principles, but they will probably try to avoid giving any more general guidance.[16]

SOME PROBLEMS WITH WORDS

The Government's reluctance may be based on much the same nervousness as was felt by the House of Lords in *Bland*: the issues are just too difficult to be confident of the right solutions. But they are also nervous of anything which might be called "euthanasia"; their further consultation upon the Law Commission's proposals will not include anything on this subject.[17] They do not explain what they mean by the term, or why they consider that it has anything to do with what the Law Commission have proposed.

"Euthanasia" is not a word known to English law. It is a Greek word derived from those for "good" (as an adjective) or "well" (as an adverb) and "death". According to the Oxford English Dictionary, it was first used in English simply to mean a quiet and easy death, then the means of procuring this, and then the action of inducing it. this last meaning is probably the one most often used today.

Until recently, as Rabbi Julia Neuberger has pointed out,[18] we had lost sight of the 18th century idea of a "good death, where farewells were said, where prayers were said, where the family came to say goodbye, and where death itself was not a terrifying presence". This was destroyed by the Victorian preoccupation

---

[14] [1990] 2 A.C. 1; see p. 24, above. Again, the Scottish courts have reached a similar conclusion by a different route: *L. v. I.'s Curator, The Times*, March 19, 1996.
[15] J. Keown, "The Law and Practice of Euthanasia in the Netherlands" (1992) 108 L.Q.R. 51; J. Griffiths, "Assisted Suicide in the Netherlands: The *Chabot* Case" (1995) 58 M.L.R. 232.
[16] See, *e.g. Re R (Adult: Medical Treatment)* [1996] 2 F.L.R. 99, p. 106, below.
[17] *Hansard* (H.C.), Vol. 269, Written Answers, January 16, 1996, col. 490.
[18] *The End or Merely the Beginning*, The 1995 Graham Lecture (1996, Counsel and Care), p. 13.

with funerals and mourning; the 20th century knowledge of the savagery of war, of the holocaust and other unimaginable horrors; and the march of medical science which turned death into a failure and tidied it into hospitals. Only recently, with development of the hospice movement, and a new interest in the social as well as the medical aspects of "going well",[19] have we begun to regain some of the old ideas.

7.34 Hospice beds[1]

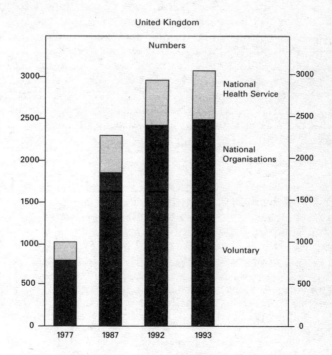

United Kingdom

1 See Appendix, Part 7: Hospice beds.

Source: Hospice Information Service, St Christopher's Hospice Social Trends 25 (1995). Crown copyright 1995 Reproduced by permission of the Controller of HMSO and the Office for National Statistics

[19] *e.g.* J. Smith, *Going Well—Six projects on death and dying assisted by the Phoenix Fund* (1995, Counsel and Care).

Some have argued that if we can regain the old idea of the good death in this way, then there will be no need or demand for the newer ideas now associated with the old word, euthanasia.[20] Even in its newer sense, the word means many different things to different people: voluntary or involuntary, active or passive. It is used to cover a good many different situations in which the law makes quite careful distinctions. These are not necessarily the right or the best distinctions, but we must begin by trying to understand them, before we can begin to work out whether or not they should be changed.

The law does not distinguish between "involuntary euthanasia" or "mercy-killing", that is killing in a kind way, but not one requested by the deceased; and "voluntary euthanasia", killing in a kind way at the request of the deceased. It does distinguish between kind killing and suicide, where the deceased kills himself, or assisted suicide, where someone else helps him to do so. It distinguishes between all of these and withholding or withdrawing life-saving treatment. Above all, it distinguishes between the deceased's own decision to refuse such treatment, whether made at the time or in advance, and the refusal of others to give it to him.

MERCY KILLING

We all have the right to go on living for as long as we want to and can. No-one has the right to take that away from us, no matter how well-intentioned their motives towards us. The exceptions to the right to life protected by Article 2 of the European Convention on Human Rights cover quite different circumstances:

"(1) Everyone's right to life shall be protected by law. No one shall be deprived of his life intentionally save in the execution of the sentence of a court following his conviction of a crime for which this penalty is provided by law.

(2) Deprivation of life shall not be regarded as inflicted in contravention of this Article when it results from the use of force which is no more than absolutely necessary:

(a) in defence of any person from unlawful violence;

(b) in order to effect a lawful arrest or to prevent the escape of a person lawfully detained;

---

[20] *e.g.* The Rt. Hon. Lord Goff of Chieveley, "A Matter of Life and Death" (1995) 3 Med. L. Rev. 1.

(c) in action lawfully taken for the purpose of quelling a riot or insurrection."

The European Commission and Court of Human Rights have not yet considered the question of euthanasia, voluntary or involuntary, under this Article. The Law Commission may be right that "in the absence of consensus in the Council of Europe on the complex moral and legal issues involved in this area it seems likely that they would show a good deal of restraint in their examination of such issues".[21]

English law draws a clear distinction between motive and intent. "Intention concerns the outcome desired as the result of an action. Motive concerns the reasons for which the outcome is desired."[22] Motive is generally irrelevant to criminal liability in English law. In *R. v. Cox*[23] a consultant rheumatologist was convicted of attempted murder for having injected potassium chloride into an incurably ill patient who died almost immediately. No-one doubted that he had acted from motives of humanity and compassion. Equally he had used a substance with no pain-killing or other therapeutic effect. It would have been different if his primary purpose had been to relieve pain. As Lord Devlin had told the jury, in the well-known case of *R. v. Adams*,[24] a doctor is entitled to relieve pain and suffering even if the measures he takes may incidentally shorten life. Dr Adams was acquitted.

In practice, we rely on the discretion of prosecutors and the sympathies of juries. Dr Cox was only charged with attempted murder, because the prosecution could not be sure that his patient had not died of her illness. Causation may offer both prosecutors and juries a merciful way out of such dilemmas. Juries are markedly reluctant to convict professionals whom they believe to have acted in good faith in their patients' interests: the best known example was *R. v. Arthur*,[25] where a paediatrician who had prescribed "nursing care only" for a severely disabled Down's syndrome baby was acquitted of attempting to murder her.

[21] Law Commission Consultation Paper No. 139, *Consent in the Criminal Law*, 1995, para. 3.29.
[22] House of Lords, *Report of the Select Committee on Medical Ethics*, Session 1993–4, H.L. Paper 21-I, para. 79.
[23] (1992) 12 B.M.L.R. 38.
[24] See H. Palmer, "Dr Adams' Trial for Murder" [1957] Crim. L.R. 365; P. Devlin, *Easing the Passing* (1985, The Bodley Head).
[25] (1981) 12 B.M.L.R. 1.

Prosecutors are bound to consider both the chances of success and the wider public interest when making their decisions.[26]

Some would argue that this is just as it should be. Merciful exceptions can be made by prosecutors and juries in individual cases without compromising the general principle that deliberate killing is wrong.[27] Professor Andrew Ashworth points out that while professionals are usually protected, such trust is not shown to relatives and friends.[28] With them, it is more likely that "legal and medical consciences are stretched to bring about a verdict of manslaughter by diminished responsibility."[29] The evidence given to the House of Lords Select Committee on Medical Ethics tends to confirm this.[30]

ASKING TO DIE

But if motive is not a legally valid distinction, what about the person's own wishes? In *R. v. Cox* there was every reason to believe that the patient wanted to be killed. A person's consent usually makes a crucial difference. It is rarely against the law to do something with the consent of the person to whom it is done. But there is one exception so large that it deprives that principle of almost all meaning in this context. Consent is in general no defence to inflicting actual bodily harm—and *a fortiori* anything worse than that—upon another person.

This principle was developed through a handful of cases beginning with duelling,[31] then prize-fighting[32] and even ordinary fist-fighting,[33] and then applied to sado-masochistic sexual practices.[34] It has not been applied to boxing, tattooing, or

---

[26] *e.g.* the decision to offer no evidence upon a charge of attempted murder against Rachel Heath, a carer alleged to have administered a fatal dose of painkilling drugs to an elderly cancer victim, was reportedly taken on public interest grounds, bearing in mind the likely penalty in the event of a conviction; see "Home help cleared of trying to murder cancer sufferer", *The Times*, March 28, 1996.

[27] *e.g.* Janet Daley, *op. cit.*

[28] A. Ashworth, *Principles of Criminal Liability* (2nd ed., 1995), p. 286.

[29] Criminal Law Revision Committee, 14th Report, *Offences against the Person*, 1980, para. 115.

[30] Report, *op. cit.*, paras. 127, 128.

[31] *R. v. Taverner* (1619) 3 Bulstr. 171, 81 E.R. 144; *R. v. Rice* (1803) 3 East 581, 102 E.R. 719.

[32] *R. v. Coney* (1882) 8 Q.B.D. 534.

[33] *A.G.'s Reference (No. 6 of 1980)* [1981] Q.B. 715.

[34] *R. v. Donovan* [1934] 2 K.B. 498; *R. v. Brown* [1994] 1 A.C. 212; see p. 98, below.

branding a man's initials on his wife's buttocks.[35] The actual rules that have developed in this area through the cases defy rational analysis and tidy codification, as the Law Commission have found.[36]

It is easy to see why duelling became unlawful: there is both a private and a public interest in outlawing the practice. There is also good reason to doubt whether all or even most participants, being driven to deliver or accept challenges by a particular code of honour, were genuine volunteers. One can even see why prize-fighting was held unlawful:[37]

"the injuries given in prize-fights are injurious to the public, both because it is against the public interest that the lives and the health of the combatants should be endangered by blows, and because prize-fights are disorderly exhibitions, mischievous on many obvious grounds."

On the other hand:[38]

"In cases where life and limb are exposed to no serious danger in the common course of things, I think that consent is a defence to a charge of assault, even when considerable force is used, as for instance in wrestling, single stick, sparring with gloves, football and the like;..."

There is an important distinction between football, in whatever form, where injuries may be caused but are not the object of the exercise, and boxing, where the whole purpose is to inflict bodily harm upon one's opponent.

The "breach of the peace" argument could not be sustained once the principle was applied to sado-masochistic practices conducted in private. There is another striking difference between these and the other cases: in duelling and fighting, including boxing, the person killed or injured does not want to be killed or injured. All he does is agree to run this risk. The masochist actively desires the sadist to hurt him. In this respect he is much more like someone who wants to be tattooed, have his body pierced or branded, or indeed to be granted a peaceful death.

The House of Lords has recently examined the principles in *R. v. Brown*,[39] which concerned sado-masochistic homosexual acts

[35] *R. v. Wilson, The Times*, March 5, 1996.
[36] Law Commission Consultation Paper No. 134, *Consent and Offences against the Person*, 1994.
[37] *R. v. Coney* (1882) 8 Q.B.D. 534, *per* Stephen J. at p. 549.
[38] *ibid.*
[39] [1994] 1 A.C. 212.

committed in private. Most of the judges discussed the issue in terms of how much harm one could consent to; should the line remain where it had previously been drawn,[40] so that one cannot consent to any actual bodily harm at all, or should it be moved to allow consent to something more serious? The majority maintained the line at any actual bodily harm. The Law Commission have since published two Consultation Papers on the subject, adopting the same basic approach, but now provisionally proposing that the line should be drawn at seriously disabling harm.[41]

However, as Lord Lane has said, the law only prohibits causing actual bodily harm, even with consent, "for no good reasons". What, then, might constitute a good reason?[42]

> "Nothing which we have said is intended to cast doubt on the accepted legality of properly conducted games and sports, lawful chastisement or correction, reasonable surgical interference, dangerous exhibitions etc. These apparent exceptions can be justified as involving the exercise of a legal right, in the case of chastisement of correction, or as needed in the public interest, in the other cases."

Although stated with great clarity, this is an extraordinarily complicated way of looking at things. Something—the hitting or the cutting—is a wrong; but then it is not a wrong if done with consent, either to the harm or the risk of harm; but it becomes a wrong again if any harm is actually done; and then it is not a wrong after all if it falls within a miscellaneous collection of exceptions. These exceptions cannot all be explained as the exercise of a legal right or needed in the public interest. It is difficult to see how it can be necessary in the public interest to allow husbands to brand their willing wives' buttocks: more plausibly it could be said that it is not necessary in the public interest to prevent them.[43]

It is not surprising, therefore, that this "quantitative-plus-exceptions" approach of the present law has been criticised as unnecessarily elaborate, leading to puzzling conclusions, placing the burden on the advocate of freedom rather than on the proponent of criminalisation, and accordingly fundamentally authoritarian.[44]

---

[40] *A.G.'s Reference (No. 6 of 1980)* [1981] Q.B. 715, C.A.
[41] Law Commission Consultation Papers No. 134, 1994, and No. 139, 1995.
[42] Lord Lane, C.J. in *A.G.'s Reference (No. 6 of 1980)* [1981] Q.B. 715, at p. 719.
[43] As indeed was said in *R. v. Wilson, The Times*, March 5, 1996, C.A.
[44] Law Commission Consultation Paper No. 139, Appendix C, para, C. 15.

On any view, however, the quantitative approach would make it impossible to consent to being deliberately killed. It is hard to see how there could ever be a compelling public interest in recognising this as an exception to the general rule, especially if sado-masochistic acts committed in private remain unlawful. If, on the other hand, the general rule were that no wrong is done to the consenting, unless there is a compelling public interest in making it so, the argument would be conducted on quite different lines.

Thus, if we were looking for exceptions to a rule which outlaws consenting to be killed, these would depend, not upon the values of the patient, but upon those of the onlooker. What level of pain or disability would be thought a good reason to allow a doctor to put a patient out of his misery? Dr Cox's patient was terminally ill and in excruciating pain. Proposals for voluntary euthanasia tend to concentrate on such cases.[45] But toleration of pain is a notoriously subjective matter. The Dutch experience has been that pain is not the most common motive for requesting help to die.[46] Again, people will vary greatly in the disabilities they will find intolerable. Paralysis and dependence on life support systems would horrify many, but others might suffer more if they became blind or deaf. And what of the patient who is not ill, disabled or in pain, but who simply finds his life intolerable?

From the outside, we might tend to say that this was not a good reason. In 1984, the British Social Attitudes survey[47] found that three-quarters of the population said "yes" to the following question:

> "Suppose a person has a painful incurable disease. Do you think that doctors should be allowed by law to end the patient's life if the patient requests it?"

Other surveys have produced similar results. But around 85 per cent said "no" to the next question:

> "And if a person is not incurably sick but simply tired of living, should

---

[45] See M. Otlowski, "Active Voluntary Euthanasia: Options for Reform" (1994) 2 Med. L. Rev. 161.
[46] Report of the Select Committee on Medical Ethics, *op. cit.*, para. 126.
[47] C. Airey and L. Brook, "Interim report: Social and moral issues", in R. Jowell, S. Witherspoon and L. Brook (eds.), *British Social Attitudes: the 1986 Report* (1986, Gower).

doctors be allowed by law to end that person's life if he or she request it?"

If, on the other hand, we were looking for reasons why procuring an outcome which the patient actively desired should be criminal, it would not matter so much what the onlookers thought of the patient's reasons. He might find his life intolerable even though other people would not. The crucial factor then would be the reality of his consent: whether he had the requisite capacity to make the choice and whether he had in fact made a real or free choice in the circumstances.

The mere fact that it is a doctor who grants the patient's request should not make any difference in principle. Diagnosing the patient's condition and giving as accurate a prognosis as possible are medical judgments. But whether either the severity of the condition or the gloom of the prognosis or any other circumstance constitutes a good reason to take the steps the patient wants must be a moral judgment.

So far, however, the law does not allow such a choice under any circumstances. In *R. v. Brown*,[48] one of the judges, Lord Mustill, rejected the "quantitative plus exceptions" approach and went looking for reasons why the consensual conduct complained of should be criminal. But even he began by saying that:[49]

"Believer or atheist, the observer grants to the maintenance of human life an overriding imperative, so strong as to outweigh any consent to its termination."

The Law Commission, in keeping to the "quantitative plus exceptions" approach of the present law, were guided by essentially pragmatic considerations, including what they called the "prevailing Parliamentary ethos". This they considered to be "redolent of a paternalism that is softened at the edges where Parliament is confident that there is an effective system of regulatory control ..."[50] Amongst the evidence for this was the unanimous view of the House of Lords Select Committee on Medial Ethics that it would be wrong to legalise "euthanasia", in the sense either of mercy killing or of complicity in suicide.[51]

[48] [1994] 1 A.C. 212.
[49] *ibid.*, at p. 261F.
[50] Law Commission Consultation Paper No. 139, para. 2.15.
[51] Report, *op. cit.*, paras. 236–41, 259–60.

It is a separate question whether the offence should amount to murder or whether there should be further categories of less culpable deliberate killings. A person who kills in pursuit of a failed suicide pact is guilty only of manslaughter;[52] the fact that he also intended to die attracts a sympathy which other mercy-killers, whether family, friend or professional, do not. If they are to remain murderers, it is also a separate question whether all should attract the mandatory penalty of life imprisonment. The "prevailing Parliamentary ethos" in the House of Lords is undoubtedly against this: two recent select committees have recommended change.[53] They are supported by many powerful voices, including the two former Lord Chief Justices.[54] However the "prevailing Parliamentary ethos" in the House of Commons is almost certainly against changing it at the moment.

SUICIDE

This leads us on to the difficult distinction between voluntary euthanasia and assisted suicide. This used not to be such a problem. The value attached to human life was so transcendant that it was a crime to try to kill oneself. This remained the law until abrogated by section 1 of the Suicide Act 1961. It is still a crime to aid, abet, counsel or procure the suicide or attempted suicide of another.[55] This offence can be committed even if the other person does not in fact kill or attempt to kill himself.[56] But there must be both the intent to assist and actual assistance. Distributing a booklet of advice on how to commit suicide can amount to this offence, provided that it was distributed to someone who was contemplating committing suicide, with the intention of helping him to do so, and that it did indeed do this.[57] Leaving the pills by the bedside can obviously do so. The fact that it is the suicide's own choice to take them in principle makes no

---

[52] Homicide Act 1957, s. 4; the burden of proof is on the defence.
[53] *Report of the Select Committee on Medical Ethics, op. cit.*, para. 261, strongly endorsing the *Report of the Select Committee on Murder and Life Imprisonment*, Session 1988–9, H.L. 78.
[54] *Report of the Committee on the Penalty for Homicide* (Chairman: Lord Lane), (1993, Prison Reform Trust).
[55] Suicide Act 1961, s. 2.
[56] *R. v. McShane* (1977) 66 Cr. App. R. 97.
[57] *A.G. v. Able* [1984] Q.B. 795, *per* Woolf J. at p. 812D–E.

more difference in this context than in any other case of assisting or encouraging crime.[58]

7.30

Death rates from suicide: by gender and age

England & Wales
Rates per 100,000 population

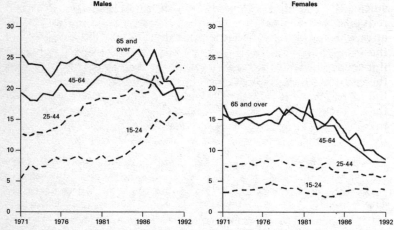

The European Commission on Human Rights has found that this offence does not violate the right to respect for private and family life protected by Article 8 of the European Convention on Human Rights:

> "While it might be thought to touch directly on the private lives of those who sought to commit suicide, it does not follow that the applicant's rights to privacy are involved. On the contrary, the Commission is of the opinion that the acts of aiding, abetting, counselling or procuring suicide are excluded from the concept of privacy by virtue of their trespass on the public interest of protecting life..."[59]

[58] *c.f. R. v. Fretwell* (1862) 9 Cox C.C. 152, considered in *A.G. v. Able* [1984] Q.B. 795, at p. 811D–G. See also J.C. Smith and B. Hogan, *Criminal Law* (7th ed., 1992), pp. 133–7.
[59] *Application 100083/82 v. United Kingdom* (1982) 6 E.H.R.R. 140, para. 13.

Meanwhile in Michigan Dr Kervorkian has twice been acquitted on charges of assisting suicide.[60] Federal courts in both Washington and New York have recently held that such an offence is incompatible with the constitutional rights of the person who wishes to die.[61] No doubt the Supreme Court will be asked to rule in due course.

Even though assisting suicide remains a crime, it carries a lesser maximum penalty than does mercy killing. Deliberately assisting suicide attracts up to 14 years' imprisonment; murder which is reduced to manslaughter because of diminished responsibility attracts up to life imprisonment, as does attempted murder; but these are maxima and much lower penalties may actually be imposed; deliberate killing with consent, however, is murder and the court has no choice but to impose the mandatory sentence of life imprisonment. Is prescribing the pills and leaving them for the patient to take[62] so morally distinct from giving the patient an injection which he wants? Especially when the reason he wants the injection is that he is unable to take the pills for himself?

GIVING UP ON OTHERS

The New York court is reported to have said that it made "no sense" that doctors could pull the plug on life support systems at the patient's request, but were not allowed to prescribe lethal doses of drugs for those who wanted them.[63] This will strike a chord with those who found it difficult to understand how the law could allow patients such as Anthony Bland, in a persistent vegetative state, to starve to death after the withdrawal of their "nutrition and hydration", but could not allow a quicker and perhaps more merciful release. Interestingly, in their evidence to the House of Lords Select Committee, the nursing profession were by no means as convinced of the validity of the distinction between "killing and letting die" as were the medical profession. Professor Sheila McClean described it as "philosophically disingenuous".[64]

Hitherto, however, lawyers have always thought that the distinction between acts and omissions made a great deal of sense.

[60] "Assisted suicide doctor cleared", *The Independent*, March 9, 1996.
[61] "US courts uphold right to assisted suicide", *The Times*, April 9, 1996.
[62] Or providing the patient with his own gas chamber, as practised by Dr Kervorkian; see *The Independent*, March 9, 1996, *loc. cit.*
[63] *The Times*, April 9, 1996, *loc. cit.*
[64] Report, *op. cit.*, paras. 69–72.

So, actively assisting suicide is different from failing to provide treatment if the patient does not want it. In the middle is withdrawing existing treatment without which the patient will die: is this assisting suicide or an invasion of his body which he is entitled to reject when he wants? The House of Lords in the *Bland* case were clear that discontinuing life support is an omission; and also that such intervention must be stopped if the patient asks. Lord Goff said plainly that "... in cases of this kind, there is no question of the patient committing suicide, nor therefore of the doctor having aided or abetted him in doing so."[65]

The distinction between acts and omissions mainly arises in the context of our duties towards other people. My legal duties are not necessarily identical to my moral duties. The law says that I must not do harm to my fellow man, either deliberately, by pushing him into the lake, or carelessly, by driving the car in which he is a passenger so badly that it falls into the lake. But I do not have to rescue him from the lake into which he has fallen of his own accord.

Some would explain this by causation: I did not cause him to fall into the lake and my failure to rescue him does not cause his death. But some philosophers would question this and causation has never been an easy subject. Others would explain it on more pragmatic policy grounds: the range of harm that can result from a failure to act is so great, and the burden of saving all the drowning people whom one could help to save so heavy, that the individual can only be held accountable if he has a specific duty to act.

That duty may be imposed by the general law in relation to particular types of people, most notably one's children, or voluntarily assumed in a particular case. We do have a duty to continue to arrange care for helpless people who may die without our help once we have begun to do so. As Sir Thomas Bingham M.R. said in the case referred to earlier,[66] "When S. suffered his stroke, it is plain that the plaintiff assumed the duty of ensuring that he was properly cared for. Having assumed that duty, she was at risk if she failed to discharge it: see *R. v. Stone*[67]." Withdrawing treatment, once begun, also has a more recognisable causal connection with the death than does the failure to treat in the first place.

[65] [1993] A.C. 789, at p. 864F.
[66] On p. 91, above: *Re S (Hospital Patient: Court's Jurisdiction)* [1996] Fam. 1, C.A. at p. 19B.
[67] [1977] Q.B. 354.

However, it is difficult to define the precise extent of a duty to provide treatment to keep people alive. It must encompass a duty to provide "basic care" for helpless people—food and drink by normal methods of feeding, hygiene and attention to normal bodily functions, but how much further does it go? A doctor does not have to provide medical treatment which would be futile or inappropriate.[68] But there is a great deal in between these two extremes. In *Re F (Mental Patient: Sterilisation),*[69] the House of Lords were discussing the justifications for providing treatment and care for people who were unable to agree to it for themselves. All the judges said that there was not only the power, but also the duty, to provide such treatment. Thus, for example, Lord Griffiths:[70]

> "In a civilised society the mentally incompetent must be provided with medical and nursing care and those who look after them must do their best for them. Stated in legal terms the doctor who undertakes responsibility for the treatment of a mental patient who is incapable of giving consent to treatment must give the treatment that he considers to be in the best interests of his patient, and the standard of care required will be that laid down in *Bolam v. Friern Hospital Management Committee*[71]."

If so, although it is said that the doctor must act in his patient's best interests, he will not be in breach of his duty if his decision not to provide treatment accords with that of a responsible body of medical opinion, however many doctors might think otherwise.

Whether or not the doctor in charge of the patient's treatment wishes to provide treatment, the decision may not be his alone. Providers of health care at public expense have to establish some priorities. The courts have held that in making individual judgments the authorities are entitled to take into account their limited resources and allocate them to best effect. The court will not force them to provide treatment, even in life and death situations. They did not have to provide a new and untried form of treatment for a child with leukaemia, even though she desperately wanted it; in fact when rather different treatment was provided

---

[68] *Re J (A Minor) (Child in Care: Medical Treatment)* [1993] Fam. 15, C.A.; see also *Re J (A Minor) (Wardship: Medical Treatment)* [1991] Fam. 33, C.A.
[69] [1990] 2 A.C. 1; also p. 24, above.
[70] [1990] 2 A.C. 1, at p. 69F–G; see also Lord Bridge, at p. 52D–E; Lord Brandon, at p. 55H–56A and p. 68C–E; Lord Goff, at p. 77D–78B–C.
[71] [1957] 1 W.L.R. 582; [1957] 2 All E.R. 118.

privately she lived happily for more than a year afterwards.[72]

The authorities do not have a completely free hand: a decision may be open to attack as so unreasonable that no properly informed and thoughtful authority could possibly make it. The classic statement of an irrational decision seems particularly fitting in this context: "It is so outrageous in its defiance of logic or accepted moral standards that no sensible person who had addressed his mind to the question to be decided could have arrived at it".[73]

Once the decision has been taken to provide intrusive life-sustaining treatment, however, it is more difficult to stop doing so. If the patient is dead, there is no need to continue to pretend that he is alive: in fact it may well be unlawful to do so.[74] If the patient is alive, however, and his wishes are not known, the *Bland* case established that treatment must, but can only, be continued if it is in his best interests.[75] The judges were clear that the question was not whether it was now in Anthony Bland's best interests for his life to be brought to an end. Instead, the question was whether it was still in his best interests to be kept alive by artificial means. In this way Lord Mustill was able to make sense of his own perception that "the distressing truth which must not be shirked is that the proposed conduct is not in the best interests of Anthony Bland, for he has no best interests of any kind."[76]

So what is the principle governing the duty to treat? Is it the best interests of the patient (as stated in the incompetence cases)? Or is it the opinion of some responsible body of doctors (the tort standard set in those cases)? Or is it the judgment of a rational health authority, with which the courts will only interfere on public law grounds (as in the provision of treatment cases)?

The recent case of *Re R (Adult: Medical Treatment)*[77] might have resolved this. Doctors had decided that a young man of 23 who was very severely disabled, both mentally and physically, should

---

[72] *R. v. Cambridge District Health Authority, ex p. B.* [1995] 1 W.L.R. 898, [1995] 2 All E.R. 129, C.A., decided on March 10, 1995; "Child B" died suddenly on May 21, 1996; P. Toynbee, "Jaymee and the final choices: The story behind the story", *The Independent*, Mary 23, 1996.
[73] *Council of Civil Service Unions v. Minister for the Civil Service* [1985] A.C. 374, *per* Lord Diplock at p. 410G.
[74] For example, by way of "elective ventilation" aimed at preserving organs for transplantation.
[75] [1993] A.C. 789.
[76] *ibid.*, at p. 897D.
[77] [1996] 2 F.L.R. 99.

not be resuscitated if his heart or lungs stopped functioning. Staff at his day care centre were concerned about this and began the process of judicial review to have the decision found irrational and unlawful on public law grounds. The next day the health authority applied for a declaration that it would be lawful and in R's best interests to withhold certain treatments in future should these become necessary. The President of the Family Division declared that he should not be resuscitated and also that it would be lawful not to give him anti-biotics if he developed a life-threatening infection, but in this case only if both the consultant and the G.P. advised this at the time and at least one of his parents consented. The test was his best interests, but as in the case of a severely handicapped baby, the court had "to judge the quality of life the child would have to endure if given the treatment and decide whether in all the circumstances such a life would be so afflicted as to be intolerable to that child".[78]

If it is difficult to understand the distinction between withdrawing feeding and giving an injection, it must be even more difficult to understand why there should be a distinction between providing artificial feeding for a patient in a persistent vegetative state, or anti-biotics for a patient in a low awareness state, and providing dialysis for a patient with kidney failure, or further chemotherapy for a child with leukaemia. One thing, however, is clear: the patient's desire to have the treatment is not the determining factor in deciding whether or not the authorities have a duty to provide it.

GIVING UP ON ONESELF

But the patient's desire not to have the treatment does determine the matter the other way about: it can relieve the authorities, not only of the duty, but also of the right to provide it. It is lawful for the person concerned to take active steps to end his own life. It is also lawful for the person concerned to refuse to accept from others what they think necessary to sustain life, including the continuation of life-support systems. Anything else would make nonsense of the requirement of consent to medical treatment. It is unlawful to force such things upon him against his will.

So much is now clear, at least for as long as the person remains

---

[78] *Re J (A Minor) (Wardship: Medical Treatment)* [1991] Fam. 33, C.A. *per* Taylor L.J., at p. 55F.

able to make up his own mind. This is what was said in *Re T (Consent to Medical Treatment) (Adult Patient)*, where a young woman had signed a form refusing blood transfusions but was now in a critical condition following an emergency Caesarian section:[79]

> "Prima facie every adult has the right and capacity to decide whether or not he will accept medical treatment, even if a refusal may risk permanent injury to his health or even lead to premature death. Furthermore it matters not whether the reasons for the refusal were rational or irrational, unknown or even non-existent. This is so notwithstanding the very strong public interest in preserving the life and health of all citizens."

The same principle was affirmed in the House of Lords in the *Bland* case, for example by Lord Goff:[80]

> "... the principle of self-determination requires that respect must be given to the wishes of the patient, so that, if an adult patient of sound mind refuses, however unreasonably, to consent to treatment or care by which his life would or might be prolonged, the doctors responsible for his care must give effect to his wishes, even if they do not consider it to be in his best interests to do so..."

Not surprisingly, doctors whose whole mission in life is to save and prolong both life and health can find this difficult to accept. They know that they have a duty of care towards their patients and that this can impose upon them a positive duty to act. But as Lord Browne-Wilkinson made crystal clear:[81]

> "The doctor cannot owe his patient any duty to maintain his life where that life can only be sustained by intrusive medical care to which the patient will not consent."

Although the cases sometimes discuss whether or not a particular procedure is medical treatment, from the receiving end there is no difference between intrusive medical treatment and intrusive methods of feeding. In *Secretary of State for the Home Department v. Robb*[82] the prison authorities wanted to know

---

[79] [1993] Fam. 95, *per* Lord Donaldson M.R. at p. 115F.
[80] [1993] A.C. 789, at p. 864C; other judges made similar observations.
[81] *ibid.*, at p. 883A.
[82] [1995] Fam. 127.

whether or not they could lawfully refrain from providing food and drink, whether artificially or otherwise, to a prisoner on hunger strike. They had in fact reached agreement with the prisoner on the declarations to be made, but the judge was asked to deliver a judgment. Long ago, in *Leigh v. Gladstone*,[83] where a suffragette had sued for damages for force-feeding in prison, the Lord Chief Justice had directed a jury that the prison authorities had a duty to preserve the health of their prisoners and that this included force-feeding them. But, said Mr Justice Thorpe,[84] "for many reasons it seems to me that that authority is of no surviving application and can be consigned to the archives of legal history."

One of these reasons was that suicide is no longer a crime. But the judge had earlier said (echoing Lord Goff in the *Bland* case[85]) that to refuse artificial feeding did not amount to suicide. We have already seen how the distinction between acts and omissions may explain this. And if refusing food is not suicide now, then why was it suicide in 1909? And if it was not suicide in 1909, why is its abolition a reason to disagree with the case? Another reason was that *Leigh v. Gladstone* was decided in the climate of dramatic conflict between the suffragette movement and the government of the day: perhaps politically controversial cases make bad law?

The judge also considered the American cases[86] which identified four "State interests" which might be balanced against the individual's right of self determination. One of these, maintaining the integrity of the medical profession, he could not recognise as a distinct consideration to be set against the individual's right to choose. And the principal countervailing interest, in preserving life, "was but part and parcel of the balance which must be struck in determining and declaring the right to self-determination".[87]

In modern English law, he decided, the right of the prisoner to determine his own future was plain. It was not diminished by his status as a prisoner. Another countervailing interest, protecting innocent third parties, could be recognised, but did not arise in this case. The last, preventing suicide, could again be recognised, but again did not arise. If this analysis is correct, therefore, only those two interests can tell against respecting a person's wish to

[83] (1909) 26 T.L.R. 139.
[84] [1995] Fam. 127, at pp. 130H–131A.
[85] [1993] A.C. 789, at p. 864F.
[86] *Thor v. Superior Court* 885 P. 2d 375 (1993), Supreme Court of California; *cf.*, *Re Caulk* 480 A2d 93 (1984), Supreme Court of New Hampshire.
[87] [1995] Fam. 127, at p. 131H.

refuse life-sustaining treatment. If so, it may still be lawful to pump out the stomach of a man who has taken an overdose, however intrusive and however contrary to his clearly expressed wishes this may be.

GIVING UP IN ADVANCE

In *Secretary of State for the Home Department v. Robb*,[88] the agreed declarations only stated that the Home Office might respect the prisoner's hunger strike for as long as he retained the capacity to refuse food and drink. Eventually he might lose that capacity.

If a person lacks the capacity to decide for himself, it was established by the House of Lords in *Re F (Mental Patient: Sterilisation)*[89] that it is usually lawful to provide whatever medical care and treatment is in his best interests. Indeed, as we have already seen,[90] there is a positive duty to do so. If the matter is indeed governed by the test in *Bolam v. Friern Hospital Management Committee*,[91] the power and duty, although covered by the same test, may not be identical in effect. The doctor is allowed to provide treatment if a responsible body of medical opinion would do so. He is also allowed *not* to provide treatment if a responsible body of medical opinion would *not* do so.

The right of self-determination would, however, be useless if it could be ignored the moment the patient became unconscious. If a patient is given an anaesthetic having consented to a particular operation, he should not be given a quite different operation unless there is some independent necessity for it. *A fortiori* he cannot be given a treatment which he has expressly declined. Lord Donaldson M.R. recognised in *Re T (Consent to Medical Treatment) (Adult Patient)* that an anticipatory refusal would be binding, provided that it was "clearly established and applicable in the circumstances".[92] On the facts of the case, however, Miss T's refusal of blood transfusions was not effective, because of a combination of her own physical and mental state and the undue influence of her mother.[93]

[88] [1995] Fam. 127.
[89] [1990] 2 A.C. 1.
[90] See p. 105, above.
[91] [1957] 1 W.L.R. 582; [1957] 2 All E.R. 118.
[92] [1993] Fam. 95, at p. 103B.
[93] *ibid., per* Lord Donaldson M.R., at p. 111E: "For my part I think there is abundant evidence which would have justified this court in substituting findings that Miss

The validity of an advance refusal was also recognised by Lord Keith and Lord Goff in *Airedale NHS Trust v. Bland*,[94] although as Lord Goff pointed out, "especial care may be necessary to ensure that the prior refusal of consent is still properly to be regarded as applicable in the circumstances which have subsequently occurred."[95]

In *Re C (Adult: Refusal of Treatment)*,[96] the patient suffered from gangrene in his foot and was advised that he stood only a 15 per cent chance of survival unless his lower leg was amputated. He refused his consent. The judge, as it happens again Mr Justice Thorpe, granted him an injunction against his ever being subjected to that treatment without his express written consent, even if he later lost his decision-making capacity.

I have heard it said that the case law is still not settled. Both *Secretary of State for the Home Department v. Robb* and *Re C* are first instance decisions, though by a highly respected judge who is now a member of the Court of Appeal, and therefore of merely persuasive authority. The observations of the higher courts in *Re T* and *Bland* are said not to form part of the essential ground for those decisions (the *ratio decidendi*) which is binding when the same point arises in the future. This is certainly true of *Bland*, because Anthony Bland had never expressed a view about what he wanted to happen. But it is hard to see what *Re T* was about if not the fundamental rule that the patient's refusal of blood had to be respected unless a reason could be found not to do so.

To me, therefore, the case law seems plain. If someone has simply not given his consent to the treatment in question, there

T was not in a physical or mental condition which enabled her to reach a decision binding on the medical authorities and that even if contrary to that view, she would otherwise have been in a position to reach such a decision, the influence of her mother was such as to vitiate the decision she expressed." Butler-Sloss L.J. would not upset the trial judge's view that she was fit to decide for herself, but held that her state of health was relevant in concluding that she was subject to undue influence which vitiated her decision. Staughton L.J. simply agreed that there was no valid refusal and that the doctors were justified in treating her by the principle of necessity.

[94] [1993] A.C. 789, *per* Lord Keith at p. 857C: "Such a person [*i.e.* who is conscious and of sound mind] is completely at liberty to decline to undergo treatment, even if the result of his doing so will be that he will die. This extends to the situation where the person, in anticipation of his, through one cause of another, entering into a condition such as PVS, gives clear instructions that in such event he is not to be given medical care, including artificial feeding, designed to keep him alive."
[95] *ibid.*, at p. 864E.
[96] [1994] 1 W.L.R. 290; [1994] 1 All E.R. 819; see also p. 27, above.

may be other justifications for giving it to him anyway. But if someone has made it quite clear that he does not want the treatment in question, then he cannot be given it at all, no matter how necessary it is in his own best interests.

Both the Law Commission[97] and the Scottish Law Commission[98] have proposed legislation on the effect of such advance refusals. The Scots could at least say that it was not possible to state their law with certainty, so that legislation might be helpful.[99] But if English law is plain, why did the Law Commission do so? They had consulted as widely as they could. Most of those who responded agreed with a provisional proposal[1] that legislation should provide for the scope and effect of anticipatory decisions. Some, however, argued that the common law could be relied upon to give adequate guidance. At first these included the British Medical Association, but in January 1994, the BMA changed its policy and decided to support limited legislation to place the law on a clear statutory basis. The House of Lords Select Committee on Medical Ethics[2] commended the development of advance directives, but did not support legislation. Others wanted legislation, not to reflect, but to reverse the present case law, so that doctors would be entitled to ignore advance refusals in certain circumstances. These responses were mainly based upon religious convictions. The BMA's guidance already points out that "if a health professional is involved in the management of a case and cannot for reasons of conscience accede to a patient's request for limitation of treatment, management of the patient must be passed to a colleague."[3]

The Law Commission, however, had no choice but to recommend legislation. The main point of the project was to develop a comprehensive scheme for taking decisions on behalf of people who are unable to take them for themselves. Part of that scheme would involve new powers for the courts to take such decisions or to appoint other people to do so. But an equally important part of the scheme is to reassure carers of all kinds that they do not have to go to court unless there is a problem. Hence

[97] Law Com. No. 231, *op. cit.*
[98] Scot Law Com. No. 151, *op. cit.*
[99] *ibid.*, para. 5.46.
[1] Law Commission Consultation Paper No. 129, *Mentally Incapacitated Adults and Decision-Making—Medical Treatment and Research*, 1993, para. 3.11.
[2] Report, *op. cit.*, para. 264.
[3] *Advance Statements about Medical Treatment*, Code of Practice, para, 13.4.

the draft Bill annexed to the Commission's Report codifies the main principle in *Re F (Mental Patient: Sterilisation)* in this way:[4]

> "it shall be lawful to do anything for the personal welfare or health care of a person who is, or is reasonably believed to be, without capacity in relation to the matter in question ... if it is in all the circumstances reasonable for it to be done by the person who does it."[5]

That person must act in what he reasonably believes to be in the best interests of the person concerned.[6] An exception to this rule therefore had to be made to cater for people who had refused their consent in advance to something the carer thought best.

A second reason for proposing legislation is that these instruments can seriously damage your health. They are not, as one respondent said, for the faint hearted. They raise practical questions which need to be clarified. Most people do not look for their law in the law reports but in legislation (where the difficult concept of *ration decidendi* does not arise). But the general approach was to preserve the rights given to the patient by the present law rather than to extend or reduce them.

Hence, the general authority to act would not apply "if an advance refusal of treatment by the person concerned applies to that treatment or procedure in the circumstances of the case."[7] The refusal could be oral or in writing and could be revoked or varied in any way and at any time while the person concerned has the capacity to do so; but unless there is an indication to the contrary a refusal is assumed to be validly made if it is in writing, signed and witnessed.[8] There would be no liability for the consequences of withholding treatment which was reasonably believed to be covered by an advance refusal; but there would also be no liability for carrying out treatment unless the doctor knew or had reasonable grounds for believing that there was such a refusal.[9] Usually, therefore, the patient would have to do something to draw the doctor's attention to the refusal; the doctor would not have to satisfy himself that there was none.

The greatest difficulty in practice is to establish whether such a

---

[4] [1990] 2 A.C. 1.
[5] Mental Incapacity Bill, clause 4(1).
[6] *ibid.*, clause 3(1).
[7] *ibid.*, clause 9(2).
[8] *ibid.*, clause 9(5), (6).
[9] *ibid.*, clause 9(4).

refusal was meant to apply to the exact situation which has arisen. The Bill affirms the bias of doctors and the law in favour of preserving life to this extent: in the absence of any indication to the contrary, the refusal will be presumed not to apply if it endangers the patient's life.[10]

The Bill contains the same presumption, also rebuttable, about a refusal which endangers the life of a pregnant woman's unborn child.[11] This would apparently reverse the effect of the decision in *Re S (Adult: Refusal of Treatment)*;[12] a pregnant woman had refused her consent to a Caesarian section, but the President of the Family Division declared that it would be lawful to perform it in the circumstances, where there was an imminent risk that both she and her baby would die. The House of Lords Select Committee on Medical Ethics[13] made no comment on this controversial decision, although they did make a plea that full reasons should always be given (which is scarcely practical if there are only 20 minutes to go before any decision will be overtaken by events).

The Law Commission did not accept that a woman's right to determine the sorts of bodily interference she would tolerate "somehow evaporates as soon as she becomes pregnant".[14] On the other hand, many women do in fact change their minds about what they will accept when they are pregnant. So a refusal which did not specifically address this point would no longer apply.

The Scottish Law Commission disagreed on this point, recommending that an advance refusal should be ineffective to the extent that it endangered the life of a foetus, aged 24 weeks or more, which the patient is carrying.[15] The law certainly recognises the interest of a viable foetus in not being deliberately harmed.[16] Yet there is a substantial difference between taking action deliberately designed to terminate the pregnancy or endanger the life of the foetus and a refusal of treatment which may have this effect. If an advance refusal of treatment can be forcibly overridden in these circumstances, it is difficult to see why a contemporaneous refusal cannot also be overridden. The Scottish Law Commission do not explain what intervention Scots Law would currently allow

[10] Law Com. No. 231, para. 5.23; Bill, clause 9(3)(a).
[11] Law Com. No. 231, paras. 5.24, 5.25; Bill, clause 9(3)(b).
[12] [1993] Fam. 123.
[13] Report, *op. cit.*, para. 235.
[14] Law Com. No. 231, para. 5.25.
[15] Scot Law Com. No. 151, para. 5,58.
[16] *A.G.'s Reference (No. 3 of 1994)* [1996] 2 W.L.R. 412, [1996] 2 All E.R. 10, C.A.

against the wishes of a pregnant woman if a doctor believes that its refusal would put the survival of the foetus in danger. *Re S (Adult: Refusal of Treatment)*[17] certainly does not go as far as that. It is not possible to use the wardship jurisdiction of the English High Court to restrict the mother's liberty for the sake of her unborn child.[18]

The interests of third parties are one of the countervailing interests which have been recognised elsewhere in the world and were accepted by Mr Justice Thorpe in *Secretary of State for the Home Department v. Robb*.[19] It might be thought quite a small step from an interest in not being harmed to an interest in obliging another person to stay alive. But it is a much greater step than it might at first seem. Enforcing this duty against the mother's wishes in an emergency such as arose in *Re S* is one thing: obliging her to accept any treatment or other restriction on her normal freedom of action which others think will benefit her baby is another. In practice, it would be extremely difficult to draw the line in the right place.

The Law Commission recommended two exceptions, where it would be lawful to give treatment despite an advance refusal. One was for treatment necessary to prevent death or serious deterioration pending a decision of the court as to whether an apparent advance refusal was in fact valid and applicable to the situation which had arisen.[20] The court would not have the power to override such a refusal, any more than it does now. But of course it should be possible to have any doubts resolved before it is too late. This exception might well apply in circumstances similar to those in *Re S*; if so, it would do less violence to the mother's rights and draw a more defensible line between acceptable and unacceptable invasions of her bodily integrity.

The other exception was for "basic care". Although this is not referred to in the case law, Professor Andrew Grubb[21] has argued that it would be contrary to public policy to require a doctor—or more realistically a nurse—to leave a patient totally unattended, even if he has asked them to do so. "Basic care" would mean keeping the patient clean, giving him food and drink by mouth, and relieving severe pain.[22]

[17] [1993] Fam. 123.
[18] *Re F (In Utero)* [1988] Fam. 122, C.A.
[19] [1995] Fam. 127; p. 108, above.
[20] Law Com. No. 231, para. 5.36; Bill, clause 9(7)(b).
[21] [1993] 1 Med. Law Rev. 84, at p. 85.
[22] Law Com. No. 231, para. 5.34; Bill, clause 9(7)(a), (8).

There is also a concern that people will make sweeping advance refusals, perhaps in very general terms, which they never revoke. It will not be clear whether this was meant to apply years afterwards to a new type of treatment for an illness they have since caught. One of the fears expressed by the House of Lords Select Committee was that to give advance directives greater legal force would "deprive patients of the benefit of the doctor's professional expertise and of new treatments and procedures which may have become available since the advance directive was signed."[23] This problem already arises under the present law. Some refusals are stated in precise and unequivocal terms: "my express refusal of blood is absolute and is not to be overridden in any circumstances." Otherwise later readers are unlikely to think that they were meant to cover new forms of life-sustaining treatment or a new set of circumstances.

This was another point on which the Scottish Law Commission differed from the English, recommending an express provision that a refusal could be disregarded if there had since been a material change in circumstances (other than in the patient's medical condition) such that the doctor reasonably believed that the patient would now accept the treatment in question.[24] The practical outcome is likely to be the same whichever approach is adopted.

Neither approach would address another concern. A person who is able to take his own decisions may be horrified at the prospect of losing that capacity and so refuse quite ordinary treatments on the ground that he would then be better off dead. Yet once he has become demented, he may be quite content; those around him who remember how he used to be will suffer much more than he does. But he will no longer be able to revoke the refusal. This, of course, is what advance refusals are all about; the right to decide while you are able to do so the extent to which you want to be obliged to stay alive. This will all depend upon what you yourself think makes life worth living: what Professor Ronald Dworkin has called your "critical interests".[25]

[23] Report, *op. cit.*, para. 264.
[24] Scot Law Com. No. 151, para. 5.53.
[25] Professor Dworkin finds the answer to this particular problem in his distinction between a person's experiential and his critical interests—the things he likes and dislikes doing or experiencing and the essence of what he considers important in life: see "Dying and Living", and "Life past Reason", in *Life's Dominion* (1993, HarperCollins).

However, many documents which are labelled "advance directives" or "living wills" do not contain a clear and unequivocal refusal of particular forms of treatment and cannot have the same legal effect. They give an indication of the sorts of treatment and management the patient would like in certain circumstances. Doctors have understandably been concerned that such a document could oblige them to carry out some positive act of treatment which they do not consider to be appropriate. A document which stated in advance which treatments the patient wanted to have would usually constitute a valid consent. But we have already seen that the law will not oblige a doctor to give treatment, even if his patient wants it, if he has formed a reasonable clinical judgment that the treatment is inappropriate or futile.[26] This sort of directive gives helpful guidance as to the patient's values and preferences, which may help the doctor to decide what will be best for him, but no more than that. It could never require or allow a doctor, or anyone else, to take positive steps to end his life.

For these reasons, an advance directive can only ever have a limited effect in law. If there is a particular treatment or procedure which you do not want under any circumstances then it will work. But you have to pick your time carefully. You must not be so close to the end that there is a risk that you will be found incapable of making such a serious choice. Equally, you should be close enough to the end to have a clear understanding of what sorts of treatment might be offered and whether or not you want them. But, as the BMA advise, you should also beware rushing into it, or acting under the pressure of an admission to hospital, or a recent diagnosis, or the influence of others.[27]

HAVING SOMEONE ELSE DECIDE FOR YOU

Most people might prefer to leave matters to their doctors anyway. Doctors should now know that the next of kin has no automatic right to decide on the patient's behalf. Both *Re T (Consent to Medical Treatment) (Adult Patient)*[28] and *Re F (Mental Patient: Sterilisation)*[29]

[26] *Re J (A Minor) (Child in Care: Medical Treatment)* [1993] Fam. 15, C.A.
[27] See BMA Code of Practice, 1995, para. 6.
[28] [1993] Fam. 95.
[29] [1990] 2 A.C. 1.

make this quite clear.[30] But relatives and friends may be very helpful in clarifying what the patient would have wanted. They may have a good idea about whether the patient would want strenuous efforts made to keep him alive after he has become demented. They may also supply important information which will help the doctor to decide what kinds of treatment will be best. The court may even conclude that it will be lawful in future to do what the doctors and the family together think best.[31] Few courts would be happy to allow the doctors to stop treating a patient if the family did not want this, even though in theory their opposition should make no difference to whether continued treatment would be best for him.

The Law Commission considered going further, but decided against this.[32] One problem with giving relatives a statutory right, either to decide or to be consulted, is that even the most sophisticated list is unlikely to come up with the right person every time. While some might want their spouses, parents or children to be consulted, this might be the last thing that others would want. If we take the definition of "nearest relative" in the Mental Health Act 1983 as an example, why should living with someone as husband and wife for a mere six months make one nearest relative, while one would have to live in a homosexual partnership for five years?[33]

Some people might prefer to appoint another person to make decisions on their behalf. This avoids some of the pitfalls of advance refusals: the appointed person would be able to take very careful account of the up to date medical advice, considered in the light of the patient's own preferences and values. But it has pitfalls of its own: the person chosen would always carry a heavy responsibility and might easily have a serious conflict of interest. The closer the connection between patient and proxy the greater those pressures and conflicts are likely to be. The lady on the next page is a striking reminder that the right person to choose then could be quite the wrong person to choose now.

At present, you can execute an enduring power of attorney, appointing an agent to look after your property and affairs after

[30] Although the doctor in *Re S (Hospital Patient: Court's Jurisdiction)* [1996] Fam. 1, C.A. said that he had been advised that the "next of kin" could decide.
[31] As happened in *Re R (Adult: Medical Treatment)* [1996] 2 F.L.R. 99; p. 106, above.
[32] Law Com. No. 231, paras. 3.33–3.36.
[33] 1983 Act, S. 26(6), (7).

By Roger Beale

you become unable to do so for yourself.[34] But this can only cover your financial and business affairs.[35] Why should you not be able to appoint an agent to look after your personal life, including your care and medical treatment as you draw near to death? The House of Lords Select Committee on Medical Ethics[36] was cautious, because the problems of pressure, burden and conflict of interest already mentioned. The Law Commission pointed out that exactly the same problems can arise now with financial decision-making:

[34] Enduring Powers of Attorney Act 1985; see Law Com. No. 122, *The Incapacitated Principal*, 1984.
[35] *Re F (Mental Patient: Sterilisation)* [1990] 2 A.C. 1, *per* Lord Brandon, at p. 59H, and Lord Griffiths, at p. 70A, on the meaning of "the affairs of patients", for the purposes of the jurisdiction of the Court of Protection under Part VIII of the Mental Health Act 1983.
[36] Report, *op. cit.*, paras, 268, 271.

they are arguments for adequate safeguards rather than prohibiting it altogether.[37]

The Commission recommended a new form of continuing power of attorney, which could cover all kinds of decision-making, personal, health and financial, depending on what the donor wanted. The donor might want the attorney to be able to make appropriate "treatment limiting decisions" at the end of life. But this is so important that it should be spelled out in the appointment. Without express authority, no attorney should have power to refuse treatment necessary to save life.[38] The same would apply to discontinuing artificial nutrition or hydration.[39] Like the patient himself, the attorney should never be able to refuse "basic care".[40]

Together, these proposals would give us some control over the manner of our passing. They would not cross the line between allowing the patient to refuse treatment and assisting him to commit suicide. They would respect the distinction between killing and letting die which the House of Lords Select Committee thought so important. Contrary to some popular beliefs, they give no more support to the legalisation of euthanasia than did the Select Committee.

PEOPLE WHO DO NOT OR CANNOT DECIDE

Even if these proposals became law, many people will never take advantage of them. People are notoriously reluctant to make wills, although less so the closer they are to death.[41] It would certainly be surprising if everyone made all the decisions which might be necessary while they were still able to do so.

At the same time, the Commission made proposals which were designed to improve the protection given to people who cannot make the decision for themselves. The case law discussed earlier[42]

---

[37] Law Com, No. 231, para. 7.7.

[38] *ibid.*, para. 7.19.

[39] *ibid.*, para. 7.18; otherwise, this would require independent authorisation by a court.

[40] *ibid.*, para. 7.16.

[41] Law Com. No. 187, *Distribution on Intestacy*, 1989, Appendix C, reports a public opinion survey conducted for the Commission. Only 33 per cent of respondents had made a will, but 60 per cent of those aged 60 and over had done so, as had 53 per cent of those in socio-economic groups A and B.

[42] See p. 105, above.

may suggest that there is at least as high a duty to provide them with treatment as there is towards capable patients. Even so, they may be more at risk from rationing decisions. Capable patients are more likely to be able to press strenuously for the treatment they want and to mobilise others to campaign on their behalf. The critical decisions will turn on the balance between the effectiveness of the treatment and the quality of life which the patient will then able to enjoy.[43] The quality of a person's life is very different indeed from the quality of the person: but at other times and other places during this century, there has been a risk that judgments about the quality of the person will lead on to the judgments about the quality of that person's life.

Another problem has been the assumption that people who cannot decide for themselves have no individual personality at all. This is obviously wrong. Even babies know what food they like and dislike. Adults who have always been mentally disabled will have a much wider range of likes and dislikes. They will also have their own attitudes towards themselves and other people, whether or not these involve anything philosophers would recognise as a moral judgment. Adults who have become disabled by illness or accident will once have had their own preferences and values. Respect for these is an integral part of respect for their best interests.

That is why the Law Commission proposed that decisions taken on their behalf should be taken in their best interests, but that this should be governed not by what a responsible body of doctors might think, but by a wider range of considerations, including the person's ascertainable past and present wishes and feelings and the factors which he would consider if able to do so.[44]

CONCLUSION

We remain nervous about respecting people's wishes at the end of life. In some ways, this is curious, because if ever there were a time when a person should be entitled to be selfish it is then. In other ways, it is not curious at all, as the penalty of getting it wrong is so serious. Although there have been criticisms of the

[43] *Re J (A Minor) (Warship: Medical Treatment)* [1991] Fam. 33, C.A.; Re. R., unreported, April 26, 1996.
[44] Law Com. No. 231, paras. 3.24–3.37; draft Bill, clause 3(2)(a); see pp. 26–27, above.

decision to impose a Caesarian section upon the mother in *Re S*,[45] few of us would have had the courage to decide otherwise. Judges do not have to make life and death decisions every day, as other professionals have to do. This is one situation in which there could be a limited obligation to stay alive.

I suggested at the outset that there was no necessary link between respecting the wishes of those who were able to decide for themselves and failing to respect the interests of those who cannot do so. We cannot be relieved our duty to care for those who cannot look after themselves. Nor am I suggesting that we should drop the crucial distinction between acts and omissions. The question is not whether someone has the right to die but whether he has a duty to stay alive which others can enforce against him.

If someone is able and free to decide for himself, and has done so, how can anyone else make the choice for him? Even his best interests depend upon what is most important to him. Some people will cling to life for as long as possible, no matter how poor its quality; some will attach far more importance to release from pain, disability or indignity. Some people will think only of themselves; some will think only of others. Some people will be guided by their religion; some will have no religion to help them. How can anyone else decide whether an atheist will fear death more or less than a committed Christian? As Mary Stott once memorably said on "Any Questions?", "it all depends in which direction you're going."

---

[45] [1993] Fam. 123; see p. 114, above.

5. Resumé

I have been exploring the balance between freedom and regulation in the three most important areas of our personal and private lives—having a child, making and breaking relationships, and ending our own lives.

A great deal has been said and written about the right to choose not to have a child. Much less has been said about the right to choose to have one. There are now three ways of going about this. You can have a child in the ordinary way; you can take over someone else's child by adoption; or you can have a child in an extraordinary way by surrogacy or assisted reproduction. Any of these can be done either inside or outside marriage.

Marriage used to be the law's way of regulating childbearing but it was always very crude. It did not insist that only good and suitable people could have children. But it did allow a father some choice in the children he would and would not recognise as his. This sort of discrimination against the innocent children who did not ask to be born is no longer allowed. The law is also beginning to make a much bigger effort to insist that all parents take some personal and financial responsibility for their children.

But the law does not try to license parents in advance. It cannot and should not try to prevent us from having children if we can. Only in very rare cases should compulsory sterilisation be allowed, and only in the best interests of a person who cannot decide for herself, not because she cannot look after a child.

But the law does not give us a right to be supplied with a child if we cannot or do not want to have one in the usual way. Buying babies from other people is forbidden. People who want to be supplied with a child by adoption are rigorously scrutinised. People who want to be helped to have a child by assisted reproduction are also scrutinised, though rather less rigorously. The supply of both is regulated with increasing care.

This is partly for the sake of the children themselves; but it is also for the sake of the whole community. We all need the next generation, but we also need it to be properly looked after and brought up. We do not want it to be designed by or for the parents' own selfish ends, any more than we would want it to be designed by or for the State.

Marriage also used to be the only way of regulating our adult relationships. It is still a very useful way of doing this, both for the couple themselves and for the whole community. But the law now allows husbands and wives a great deal of freedom to arrange their lives in whatever way seems best to them. It no longer insists, if it ever did, that men and women adopt particular roles within the relationship. It tries to give them equal status. But it also tries to redress any disadvantages which the relationship has brought to one or the other. It insists that they have certain responsibilities towards one another which should be acknowledged if their relationship comes to an end.

The Family Law Act 1996 reinforces this approach. The present divorce law is dishonest and confusing. It pretends to be based on the "no-fault" principle that the marriage has irretrievably broken down but retains the possibility that one party can blame the other for the breakdown. This too is a pretence as neither in principle nor in practice can the courts decide who was really at fault. But it does offer them both a quick way out of one marriage and into another, often before their responsibilities towards one another and their children have been properly defined. The new law would insist that they both pause for thought and make the necessary arrangements for discharging their present responsibilities before they are free to take on new ones.

Despite the flexibility and equality of the modern law of marriage, more and more young people are choosing not to marry at all, whether or not they have children together. The law no longer lets these couples avoid their responsibilities towards their children. It is also beginning to acknowledge that they may have voluntarily undertaken responsibilities towards one another. But it is taking longer to work out whether it should make them undertake more. Sooner or later the same issues will arise between same sex couples, whether or not they also have children.

The younger generation welcome the changing style of personal relationships. They are unlikely to be willing to return to the rigidity and inequality of the old law. But this does not mean that they should be able to make and break their relationships without thought for the consequences either for one another or for their children.

The law is more reluctant to allow us to choose when and how we will die. Yet we hardly ever owe a duty to anyone else to stay alive. And it cannot always be in our own best interests, or in those of the whole community, to be kept alive indefinitely. So why does the law not allow us to make our own decisions about these matters? This question raises the most acute moral problems of all, yet Parliament is unlikely to provide us with any clear answers in the near future. The case law therefore needs careful analysis.

Once again, the dividing line seems to be between people who can make their own arrangements and people who need help from others to do so. We are allowed to take our own lives. We are also allowed to refuse to accept medical treatment which we do not want. We can even do this is advance, before we become unable to choose for ourselves. We cannot yet appoint another person to choose on our behalf what treatment to accept or reject, but perhaps one day we will be able to do this.

But we cannot insist on being given any particular type of treatment if the doctors do not think it right. We cannot ask other people either to help us to take our own life or to take it for us. Sometimes others find it difficult to see the difference between killing and letting die; sometimes it can seem insensitive or even cruel. But in law it is still the crucial distinction between what we are and what we are not allowed to do with our own lives and is likely to remain so.

The new balances between choice and regulation are only slowly emerging. The law cannot impose a dictatorship, however benevolent, which insists that it knows best how people should conduct their private and family lives. It is certainly not going to persuade the younger generation to go back to the old ways of doing things. But that does not mean that everyone has to be supplied with the means of doing things differently. Nor does it mean that choices can be made irrespective of the consequences for the other people involved. New possibilities in human life and relationships are emerging all the time and the law will have to stay alert to develop in response to them.